12 LESSONS IN BUSINESS LEADERSHIP

This book is loaded with practical business advice and real-world examples. I challenge the business reader to look seriously in the mirror as to how they are leading their teams. One of my companies had 2,600 salespeople, but I would regularly state that there weren't 2,600 best ways to sell our products. Better to figure out the one best way, practice the best way, and increase the probability of success. All too often we get distracted from the basics and preparation by the urgencies of the day. Effective leaders stay committed to what is important and enjoy consistent success. The 12 important lessons in business leadership delivered here, when consistently followed, will distance you from the competition.

There's nothing difficult here. It fundamentally comes down to execution. That is leadership!

—Jack Daly
CEO, Coach, Speaker, and Author
www.JackDalySales.com

Introduction

While writing this book, many friends asked, "Why are you writing a *business* book about Tom Brady? He's an *athlete*." Some asked the more critical question, which is, "Why are you writing about Tom Brady *at all?*" They knew neither of us are Patriots fans—or fans of Boston (or Tampa) sports in general. In fact, we both celebrated with the rest of the country when Eli Manning led the New York Giants to beat Brady's New England Patriots twice in the Super Bowl. Worse yet, Kevin was an Oakland Raiders season ticket holder during the "Tuck Rule Game." And to be perfectly honest, we both much prefer baseball, despite our endless argument over whether the American League plays *real* baseball with designated hitters (Kevin is a National Leaguer all the way).

Ahem . . . back to Brady and business leadership.

Now more than ever, companies demand more productivity and leadership from their employees. Modern technology creates some efficiency and makes advanced soft skills a nice idea, but technology doesn't inherently make better leaders, and there are few good bosses with the time and constructive knowledge to guide the way for up-and-comers. Sadly, many of even the best business schools lack useful courses in leadership.

In our media interviews with more than 300 CEO members of YPO (formerly Young Presidents' Organization), the number-one complaint was the lack of leadership capability among employees. This often results in slower growth for the company and a disappointing career trajectory for the employee. But whose fault is it really? Executives can't expect leadership from those with inadequate training and a lack of good role models in their own supervisors. Most employees have yet to receive help with the skills they need to succeed personally, not to mention an understanding of how to get the best out of others.

To help those employees, wouldn't it be great to analyze the strong leadership abilities of a successful public figure, and translate them into accessible, practical lessons? Better yet, share those examples through the vivid drama the sports lens provides?

Enter Tom Brady, the winningest quarterback in NFL history and a fixture in sports and pop culture. Love him or hate him, Brady led the New England Patriots on one of the most impressive and unlikely dynastic runs in the history of professional sports. No team gets there without a leader of immense skill. For all his obvious flaws, and as much as at times it may pain us to admit, Brady is indeed such a leader.

We are writing about Brady because we are students of leadership. Revered or hated by fans, he is loved and respected by those who work with him, and even his harshest critics cannot deny his abilities and leadership success.

Now, we are well aware of the arguments that Tom Brady is not perfect, and we are definitely not here to hero-worship him. Like any leader, he's made plenty of mistakes, and there will be those who forever view him as a cheater. This book is designed not as a tribute to Brady, but as an extraction and catalogue of the leadership insights from his public behavior on and off the field. Brady continues to inspire those around him, regardless of public opinion and scrutiny. The fact that he can continue to lead at such a high level while under today's spotlight of critical mass media may in itself represent a key talent to his success.

Examining the inner workings of Brady's leadership methodology is a bit of a challenge. It's extremely difficult to break past the media embargo of the NFL and Patriots to get the inside scoop. Luckily, there are plenty of public stories about Brady and his leadership approach from which to extract information. We scoured history and selected football events and actions that richly demonstrate leadership highlights from Brady. The stories in this book are based on real events, but in many cases we created unnamed characters or fictionalized real scenarios to bring Brady's style to life. We have done our best to expose his abilities from the beginning of his career through his Patriots tenure, which ended after the 2019 season.

We have set up the book with stories of Brady's leadership, followed by commentary on the lessons learned. Then we provide real stories of business leaders who exemplify (or sometimes fail at!) similar practices. Finally, we provide actionable steps so you can execute those leadership plays in your world, over and over again.

To best use this book, read a chapter at a time. They are written to stand on their own and order does not matter. Read it all the way through or reference the lesson that helps you when you need it most. Contemplate the stories, absorb the lessons, and practice the skills until you are able to execute and lead like a champion each and every week.

Now go enjoy, learn, and win!!

—Kevin and Anne Mary

PART I
Managing the Clock

CHAPTER 1

Create a Winning Playbook

"Study your playbook."[1]
—Tom Brady, commenting on a rookie teammate's Instagram post

MAKE YOUR WEAKNESS WORK FOR YOU

Tom Brady will go down in history as one of the best quarterbacks ever to play in the NFL. He's a superstar of the highest order, a six-time Super Bowl champion, and a first-ballot Hall of Famer. He's the All-American Golden Boy. With all he's accomplished, it would be easy to assume that his success was predestined and long predicted, that he's fulfilling the great promise he showed from his earliest days. But truth, as they say, is stranger than fiction, and it's no different with Tom Brady.

Brady grew up in the shadows of his more athletic older sisters, and was known as "Maureen Brady's little brother."[2] He never played organized football until high school. There wasn't much athletic about him, and he was among the slowest guys on the team.[3] If anyone ever paid attention to him in sports, it was on the baseball diamond as a right-handed catcher who hit left-handed.[4]

It's unlikely anyone could foresee Brady's future football dominance—except for Brady himself. As a kid, he wrote an essay claiming that one day, he would be a household name, the well-known Brady of the family.[5] It must have struck those around him as a delightfully childlike fantasy. No one but Brady could have known it was prescient.

For a long time, the doubters, even the loving ones, were right. As a freshman in high school, he was the backup quarterback on a freshman team that went 0–8–1 and didn't score a single touchdown.[6] He didn't make the varsity team until his junior year.[7] Similarly in college at the University of Michigan, he didn't start until his junior year, and even then had to fight off fierce competition for the job.[8] Brady got little attention from NFL scouts, and wasn't drafted until the sixth round. He began his professional career as the backup to well-established star Drew Bledsoe. Certainly this couldn't be the career arc of a guy who would go on to win six Super Bowls, right?

In hindsight, there were signs—even if they weren't obvious at the time—that Brady would achieve beyond the indications of his natural skill. It was clear Brady was motivated, and the speed bumps he encountered only made him more so. Even after 20 years in the NFL, he still plays like a guy who has something to prove to his doubters. Further, Brady always worked hard on the mental and physical aspects of the game. His work ethic was and is legendary.

The most telling thing of all, however, was that Brady had a plan, and he worked it. Playbooks are the foundation of every football team, and Brady is no exception. Those who analyze business leadership would say he developed his own personal playbook to put himself in the best position to lead and win. Brady's playbook maximized his strengths, minimized his weaknesses, and managed his time so he could exemplify the highest standard and still have time to lead his team through anything. It's a playbook he still uses today.

The first element of Brady's playbook is his strict daily routine. It defines his day-to-day and impacts every part of his life, personally and professionally. Brady wakes up at the crack of dawn every morning and goes to bed at 8:30 p.m. every night.[9] In between, he follows a highly structured plan. His consistent schedule means his team, his family, and his business associates all have reasonable expectations of his availability and know when he will devote time to them. During those times, Brady can be fully present and engaged because he doesn't need to worry about other things—they're already squared away as a result of his regular schedule. Brady's routine sets up everything else in his life, both personal and professional.

The second part of Brady's playbook is about getting himself into peak physical condition. A leader must walk his talk, and Brady never failed in this. For example, he never shied away from the truth about his speed. His high school coach, Tom MacKenzie, said, "Most teenagers will avoid at all cost what they aren't good at. Tom Brady was the opposite. He'd take to heart what he needed to improve on."[10] In what became typical Brady fashion, he attacked his speed problem with vigor, going so far as to spray paint his parents' backyard patio so he could do the five-dot speed and footwork drill at home.[11] He developed a jump rope routine that MacKenzie incorporated into the team conditioning program.[12] He stayed after practice to do more throwing work.[13]

Over time, the physical elements of Brady's playbook evolved. He swears by his TB12 Method's focus on what he calls muscle pliability, which he claims makes muscles long, soft, and resilient,[14] prepared to take hits and recover quickly. Brady doesn't spend time at the gym sweating to increase his bench press or improve his sprinting splits. He spends his workout time focusing on things that will measurably contribute to his team's success on the field. Brady is also famously maniacal about his diet, which he believes helps him perform at his physical best. He doesn't eat tomatoes, and he "indulges" in a frozen avocado concoction he refers to as "ice cream."[15] By prioritizing and using wisely the time he spends on his physical conditioning, he can hold others accountable on their workouts and can create the time necessary to do other preparatory work.

The next part of Brady's playbook is mental preparation. He never shortchanges his preparation. No matter the game, no matter his familiarity with the opponent, no matter how great the team around him or how terrible the opposition, Brady's mental approach doesn't vary. Studying film allows him to identify every wrinkle a defense can present to him. It reveals the tendencies and preferences of opponents and uncovers their weaknesses. This allows him to do better pregame planning and make better decisions at the line of scrimmage.

As with the physical requirements, the mental elements of Brady's playbook evolved over time, too. In college, he worked with assistant athletic director Greg Harden and learned the importance of visualizing his end goal and creating a step-by-step process to get there.[16] He stopped worrying so much about how others played and instead focused on his own performance. Together, Brady and Harden tackled Brady's motivation, self-belief, and internal reactions.[17] Brady learned to control everything he was able to by developing solid routines that went beyond conditioning and film study.[18]

Today, Brady also incorporates brain training into his playbook. He plays brain games every day to keep his mind in peak condition, increase processing speed, improve decision-making, and boost focus.[19] His preparation allows him to recall quickly and clearly what he learned in film sessions and team meetings. He instantly diagnoses defenses and can change the play call or adjust how his linemen protect him. By devoting himself to mental preparation, Brady can spot problems sooner and solve them more easily. He's also better able to keep his team aligned and lead them through any crises that may arise. The time Brady spends in preparation enables him to be more efficient during the game.

The last part of Brady's playbook is the play scheme he developed with head coach Bill Belichick and offensive coordinator Josh McDaniels. Brady may not be the most athletic football player of all time, but he's maximized the physical gifts he does have. In fact, the scheme even emphasizes Brady's speed—just not foot speed. Instead, their playbook relied on Brady's fast analysis of the defense and his quick release of the ball. His instant recognition of defenses—enabled by his mental preparation—allows him to know where he's going with the ball before it's even snapped. And his quick release of the ball—enabled by his physical preparation—means that the play is more likely to be successful, and that he is less likely to get hit. The proof of that is in the numbers: Brady's sack rate in 2018 was 4 percent, while the average across the league was almost 8 percent.[20] Getting pressured less and hit fewer times means Brady makes fewer rushed decisions, suffers fewer injuries, and sustains fewer concussions. He's on the field, playing healthy and at his sharpest, and keeping consistency for his team. The physical and mental preparation that are fundamental parts of Brady's personal playbook all come together in his team's actual playbook.

LEADERSHIP LESSONS FROM THE FIELD:

- Great leaders are highly aware of their own flaws and aren't afraid to admit them. Their goal is to understand the problem so they can solve it, thereby making their teams better.
- Leaders must use their time wisely. No one can be great at everything, so a leader must choose what is most important for the team's success.
- The best leaders develop a personal playbook, including a daily routine that organizes their time efficiently. Playbooks maximize their strengths, compensate for their weaknesses, and allow them the time they need to manage the team and overcome obstacles.

COMPANIES NEED PLAYBOOKS, TOO

Sports teams aren't the only organizations that need playbooks. Startup entrepreneurs and executives often run the company by the seat of their pants. It's not because they have bad business acumen, but rather because there is so much to do and limited resources with which to do it. For a while, it can work, since smaller companies are better able to adjust to changing conditions. Eventually, however, that approach becomes unsustainable and stunts growth. It's possible even Brady himself was happy to rely on his rocket arm until he realized how his foot speed was holding back his play.

Playbooks offer a critical tool for leaders to guide business teams. As teams grow, the team makeup changes from a few generalists to a lot of specialists. Large companies have many moving pieces that must coordinate to perform well. Without a playbook to guide and synchronize, goals become much more difficult to accomplish. Playbooks show how the game is played, explain the rules, give instructions, and share best practices. They also define how different business units should work together and what the problem-solving process looks like.

Playbooks also help leaders implement best practices, update procedures, and increase efficiency. High-performing organizations are nearly 80 percent more likely to prioritize sales playbooks.[21] Companies with playbooks average 39 percent stronger year-over-year increases in deal sizes than companies who don't use them.[22] Yet stunningly, only around 45 percent of organizations use playbooks.[23]

Brady's playbook determines his daily schedule, details his physical and mental workouts, and explains how he performs within the team. A company playbook needs to be similarly thorough and should encompass sales, operations, onboarding, and all other regular needs. For example, the sales section of a playbook should include a detailed breakdown of the sales process and what the sales representative should do at each step. It should be comprehensive, starting with generating a lead and continuing all the way through to maintaining a strong relationship even after the deal is closed. The sales section should provide a script for reps to use with clients at each stage of the sales process and include the best answers to the most frequent questions and objections from customers.

The operations section of a playbook explains how projects get completed and how various divisions communicate. It sets up procedures that keep the company running smoothly, addresses client concerns quickly, and anticipates problems. It even gets into detailed issues such as the proper way to complete and submit paperwork. The onboarding section of a playbook is fundamental because it's where each employee begins their understanding of how the company works. Just as it does for a sports team, a playbook keeps a company well functioning and successful.

ACTION FROM THE BUSINESS STADIUM: SELLING CUSTOMERS ON YOUR PLAYBOOK

Business coach Dan Larson, coauthor with Jack Daly of the bestselling book *The Sales Playbook: for Hyper Sales Growth*,[24] shared his experience on the critical importance of playbooks in the business world. One client, Aaron, who owned a holding company, just acquired a company and hired Dan to turn around the sales department.

"Dan, I need your help," Aaron began. "I'm an experienced businessman. I've founded and taken two companies from nothing into industry leaders, turned around several others, and successfully scaled even more. But I just can't crack this nut," he lamented. Like Brady, Aaron wasn't too proud to recognize his shortcomings. He knew he needed to identify the problem so he could fix it and improve company performance.

"The company sells advertising space," Aaron continued. "You know, billboards, stadium screens, things like that. They have a good product, and I got a great deal on it —but that's because it's hemorrhaging money. There are two sales VPs and 350 salespeople across the country, and they're losing two million dollars a year. I've been studying the business and the industry, but I haven't figured the way out yet."

"OK, Aaron, happy to help," Dan replied. "Give me thirty days to examine the company, conduct interviews, and get the lay of the land. Then we identify the problems and explore solutions."

Over the next month, Dan took a deep dive into the company. He found many good fundamentals: the industry was growing, the company had good products and strong relationships, and the salespeople were motivated. But he uncovered a number of alarming realities as well. The sales division was broken down into five regions across the country, and there was no cohesion among them. If one region found something that worked, the other regions never heard about it. It wasn't out of greed or rivalry, but simply out of a lack of communication channels. When Dan held interviews with them, the two vice presidents of sales seemed to say all the right things, but didn't seem to do many of them. They claimed to be very hands-on with the mid-level managers and salespeople, but they spent more time wining and dining clients than coaching their people. They also said they were open to new ideas, but every time Dan suggested changes, they claimed they were impossible to do, or simply didn't act on them.

After a thorough assessment, Dan was ready to present his findings to Aaron. Dan shared the good things he found, but spent more time on the issues he uncovered.

"Unfortunately, your biggest problems are your two sales VPs," said Dan. "Sorry to be so frank but they're ... useless. They make enormous salaries, don't coach their teams, never set up best practices, and are totally resistant to change. Now, it's true they're good salesmen. But instead of teaching the effective methods they've developed, they're letting the reps spin their wheels with ineffective approaches, and then they sometimes swoop in as heroes. The VPs aren't using their time well, and it's holding back all the reps from using their time well. They're a burden, not an asset."

"They've been with the company a long time," Aaron responded. "I'd hate to see morale fall because I dismiss such longtime employees and make everyone else nervous."

"That may happen in the short term, but it won't last," Dan asserted. "Getting rid of these two guys is going to liberate your salespeople to do their jobs way better and way more efficiently. It's addition by subtraction."

"So what do you suggest?" asked Aaron.

"Let's replace them with one VP of sales. It's all you really need, if that person's effective. While starting a trial with that person, I'd like to begin a pilot program in one of the five regions that I think will totally turn around the entire department," Dan said.

"Who would we put in the VP role?" Aaron followed up.

"We want someone who understands sales, but who is willing to try a different approach. Someone who's coachable and has the skill to execute a plan. Actually, I have someone internal in mind," smiled Dan.

Dan then shared his view that Charlie, a team leader in the Southeast sales region, was the right person for the job. Just as Tom Brady slaved over five-dot and jump rope drills, Charlie did everything he could to keep himself in top sales team leadership shape. He pored over industry research, read books on leadership and team building, and sought feedback. Also like Brady, Charlie demonstrated strict time management with his rigid daily schedule, so he could use all remaining time to lead and support his team. During their interviews, Charlie peppered Dan with questions about how he could serve his team better and was clearly a creative problem solver. Charlie understood the ethos of the company and what they were trying to build, and he was excited about exploring new approaches to sales.

Aaron was intrigued, unaware that he had a rising star on his hands. He decided Dan's plan was the best way forward, so he removed the existing VPs and named Charlie as their replacement. Then Dan went to work with Charlie to implement the pilot program in the Southeast region.

Together, Dan and Charlie crafted a sales playbook for their representatives. It wasn't comprehensive—after all, they had a limited time to prepare it, and sales had to continue while they implemented the new program. Still, the playbook encompassed the basics. Dan and Charlie created a script for sales representatives to use during introductory calls, follow-ups, and deal closings. They listed proper responses to customers' most frequent objections. They produced standard sales materials for all sales reps to use, instead of relying on reps to craft bespoke materials for each lead. Dan and Charlie also worked with mid-level sales team managers to improve their leadership skills and develop a stronger sense of teamwork.

It wasn't a perfect solution. Dan knew that in the long term, the company would need to incorporate more information into the sales scripts and objection response documents, as well as create a large-scale leadership development program. Still, Dan believed that even these initial steps, along with Charlie's skills and enthusiasm, would make a difference in the region. With Dan's guidance, Charlie introduced the playbook within the region and assisted the team leaders in implementing them.

The sales representatives in the Southeast region seemed to take to the program well. With standardized sales materials ready to use with any client, the reps could spend more time developing leads and building relationships. Further, with ready-made responses to client objections, they no longer had to search within the organization for answers, allowing them to close more deals faster. Brady's personal playbook evolved over time as he learned more and developed skills. Similarly, as they received feedback from managers and sales reps, Dan and Charlie adjusted and expanded their sales playbook.

About 45 days after their meeting to discuss solutions, Aaron called Dan.

"Dan, what the hell did you do to the Southeast division?" Aaron began.

"Um . . ." Dan responded, perplexed by the apparent anger in Aaron's voice. "We developed a playbook for the sales reps to use and worked on leadership development skills with the managers. It's not a comprehensive program yet, but it's a framework for one. Is there a problem?"

"Problem?" Aaron repeated. "I guess I'm not sure. I'm looking at last month's numbers for the Southeast, and it seems like they can't be right. It was the best month in the region—actually, the best month in the company—in two years. I'm stunned."

"Well that's great!" enthused Dan, now understanding Aaron's tone. "A playbook is a powerful tool."

"Dan, these numbers are unbelievable. I don't care if the playbook isn't finalized yet—I want you to implement it right away in every region. We've got to get this thing into the hands of our sales reps across the country!" demanded Aaron.

With that, Dan went to work with Charlie to install the company playbook across all the regions. As they learned more about the regions, discovered useful tools individual teams used, and picked up on nuances unique to certain types of customers, they incorporated all that information into the playbook. Dan, Charlie, and Aaron worked together to develop a comprehensive leadership development program that would begin as soon as a new team member was hired.

Within four months of their initial meeting, the company went from an annual $2 million deficit to fully in the black. The marketing company continued to grow and is still growing even several years later. Their sales playbook transformed the company into a juggernaut, just as Brady's playbook helped lead the Patriots to consistent championship performance.

GAME REVIEW:

- Leaders who use their time wisely enable their team members to do the same.
- Playbooks develop over time. Even the best leaders don't have all the answers immediately. They codify as much useful information as they can and constantly search for ways to improve their own performance and playbook.
- Great leaders don't need to be heroes. They hold themselves to the very highest standards, but they understand their most important job is not their individual performance. Instead, they focus on how their actions demonstrate best practices and create the time needed to lead the team to victory.

EXECUTING THE PLAY

Exercises for the Preseason:

- Examine the operations procedures within your team. Which processes work well, and which create bottlenecks? How much more could you and your team accomplish if those tasks could be completed more efficiently? What challenge would you be able to tackle with that extra time?

- For a deeper dive into developing a sales playbook, read *The Sales Playbook: for Hyper Sales Growth* by Jack Daly and Dan Larson. They explain how sales managers and representatives can work smarter and grow more efficiently.

Best Practices for the Game:

- Create a personal playbook for yourself. It's tough to lead others when you are off track and distracted. Establish your personal objectives for physical, mental, and material goals. Then reverse engineer a path for achievement. Enlist peers and coaches as necessary. For success tools, go to KevinDaum.com/success.

- Create an operations playbook for your leadership position. Consider the key functions you fulfill, how you interact with people in other divisions, and what your daily schedule includes. Identify places where you can boost your performance and help your team. Then create a plan to realize those improvements.

CHAPTER 2

Make Time Your Ally

"I got a chance to hold my draft card a few hours ago.
Never forget where you came from."[1]
—Tom Brady

EARLY BIRD WITH A PLAN

Rodney Harrison was a paragon of professionalism. In his standout collegiate career at Western Illinois University, he earned defensive back records of 345 career tackles and 28 tackles in a single game.[2] Harrison was a Second Team All-American in 1992, and the following season was named First Team All-American by five different organizations. He was drafted by the San Diego Chargers in 1994, and would go on to become the first player in NFL history to record 30 sacks and 30 interceptions in his career.[3] His teammates selected him to receive the Ed Block Courage Award, given each year to the player who best exemplifies the principles of courage and sportsmanship while also serving as a source of inspiration.[4] When he finally retired in 2009, he was the NFL's all-time leader in sacks by a defensive back.[5]

So when he arrived in New England in 2003, Harrison was already a standout in the locker room and on the field. He had been to two Pro Bowls and was still in the prime of his career. In his years of professional experience, he learned what was required for sustained, high-level success. He was a poster child for a relentless, aggressive work ethic.

In New England, Harrison met his work ethic spirit animal in Tom Brady. The scenario may have gone something like this:

Harrison was regularly up and at 'em early while in San Diego, and it was no different on his first day with the New England Patriots. Braving the bitter Massachusetts cold, he arrived at the practice facility at 6:30 a.m. and walked into the dark lobby. As always, it was an odd feeling to be alone in a building normally full of huge, passionate football players and loud, demanding coaches. A building usually so vibrant and alive was dark and silent.

But then—*was that a noise?*

Harrison wasn't sure. He wasn't used to the Patriots' facilities and the noises of the building. He didn't know the building maintenance schedule. *Who else could possibly be here this early? Was the overnight cleaning crew not finished yet?*

He heard it again.

Now his curiosity was piqued. Harrison followed the noise down the hall. It got louder as he turned a corner. He closed in on it as he approached the team gym. The lights were on. Someone was definitely in there. Harrison couldn't believe it. He peeked in, and there appeared a solitary figure: Tom Brady, mid-workout. Harrison was speechless. *What time did Brady get here? It's six-thirty a.m. He lives forty-five minutes from the facility, yet he's already here and working up a lather.* Brady looked up.

"Good afternoon!"[6] Brady yelled and smiled, clearly amused by Harrison's stunned look. Once he got over his shock, Harrison laughed. Who knew the Golden Boy could be funny? Harrison greeted Brady and got ready for his own workout. Harrison could still hardly believe anyone would arrive earlier than he did, but it was nice to have a teammate with him, putting in the hard work no matter the time of day.

The next day, the same thing happened. When Harrison arrived at 6:30 a.m., there was Brady, mid-workout, greeting Harrison with another, "Good afternoon!" But when Harrison arrived on the third day, there was no noise in the building. *Got him*, Harrison smiled. He walked his normal route down the hall, passing the gym. And indeed, the gym was dark and silent. No Brady. Harrison understood. *Yeah, Brady has a Super Bowl ring, but the guy's twenty-five years old. No one at that age has the discipline to maintain a routine like mine, especially at such ungodly hours. They just don't understand yet how important it is.*

But on his way to the locker room, Harrison noticed a faint light emanating from a meeting room at the end of the hallway. *Couldn't be,* he thought. Harrison continued down the hall and looked in. And there was Brady, watching game film, with several pages of notes already. Noticing the movement, Brady turned around in his chair, waved, and said,

"Good afternoon!" Again, Harrison was stunned. Brady was there again, well into his work before Harrison even arrived.

Now Harrison wanted to try an experiment. Surely no one, not even Brady, could get there earlier than Harrison when he really put his mind to it. Over the course of the next few weeks, Harrison started arriving at the team facilities earlier and earlier in the morning. Somehow, Brady was always there first. It became a running joke between the two: no matter how early Harrison got there, he would find Brady, already mid-workout or deep into a video session. And every morning, Brady would wish Harrison a hearty, "Good afternoon!"

Eventually, Harrison had to relent.

"Man, I don't give a damn what you say, Tom, I'm not coming in earlier than 5:30!"[7]

Harrison learned what fellow Patriots already knew: Tom Brady is maniacal about his daily routine. It's a critical part of his playbook (see Chapter 1). Some people may consider Brady's daily routine . . . quirky. He claims to wake up without an alarm clock and go to bed at 8:30 every night. His workouts consist largely of exercise with resistance bands. In reality, it almost doesn't matter what Brady's day-to-day schedule is. What's important is that it works for him, and he's devoted to it. In a larger context, it allows him the time he needs to align his team around the ultimate prize: winning championships.

Brady uses his daily routine to take tangible steps towards his long-term goals. The most powerful thing about his schedule is the time it allows him to be a great leader. He used this approach as far back as high school. His dedication to his five-dot drill, jump rope routine, and extra throwing sessions prepared him for game day. This guaranteed he had the time to invite his teammates over for extra film study. As Brady's mom made them lunch, he would point out what he saw on tape, make suggestions, and ask questions.[8] Beyond setting a good example, Brady's time management means he has time to align everyone else towards efficiency, too, and keep them on track to a championship.

Brady's professional career demonstrates the same smart use of time. By arriving early, managing his workout routines, and eating food that makes him feel good, Brady is allowing himself time to fulfill extra duties. He's able to put in extra throwing sessions with new receivers to help develop their timing. He can spend time in the film room with a tight end who had a poor showing. He can take his offensive line out to dinner to thank them for protecting him in the game. Part of what makes Brady such a good leader is his ability to put in all the extra time with his team. Developing the skills of his teammates, improving their performance, and building team camaraderie all move the team closer to championship level.

LEADERSHIP LESSONS FROM THE FIELD:

- Leaders broadcast a clear goal which the team works towards every day, in actions large and small. Leaders inspire each member of the team to focus intensely on the same vision.
- Great leaders create daily schedules that keep them in full command of all their responsibilities. Their routines reflect the same priorities identified in the team's playbook.

(Continued on next page)

• A leader who uses their own time wisely has the power to help teammates do the same. The best leaders invest quality time in their teams, individually and as a group. That time keeps people aligned behind the ultimate goal and ensures projects stay on track.

ALIGN YOUR TEAM EFFICIENTLY WITH LONG-TERM PLANNING

Tom Brady plays football to win Super Bowl championships. Brady has a crystal clear vision of the future, and he ensures that everything he and his teammates do works towards that goal. Like Brady, business leaders need to envision and articulate their preferred future and rally their teams around that goal. Many business leaders struggle to make time for long-term planning. Understandably, they get caught up in the "doing." There are so many day-to-day tasks to complete, fires to put out, and projects to steer. It can be overwhelming. To stay on track, Brady carefully crafted his daily schedule to allow him to get everything done—and then he sticks to that schedule. He uses his time efficiently and then helps his team do the same. Business leaders should model their time management after Brady's.

Brady is also a master at goal setting. Generally, people with specific goals are ten times more likely to achieve success.[9] Effective business leaders schedule their time so they have full control over their regular tasks and a complete understanding of the team's status. This leaves the leader time to dig into problems that any team members are having and time to identify and improve inefficiencies in team processes. The leader can also use the time to build team cohesion and even to develop leadership skills in teammates. Brady and other effective leaders also ensure the team understands the critical role each person plays in the process as a whole. They make sure every teammate sees how the small steps come together to make large strides. Engaged leaders ensure that every member of the team is on the same page, working towards the same goal in the same way.

Leading a team to victory requires a leader who can take an abstract idea and get it to completion. To achieve something great, you can't take a haphazard approach. Like Brady, the best leaders leave little to chance. Erratic firefighting sucks up valuable time and resources. Instead, strong leaders develop a step-by-step plan to get the team there. Inadequate and inconsistent planning creates confusion and distraction, often resulting in missed milestones and frustration. That's why effective leaders develop plans carefully and work those plans systematically. Ultimately, a leader's mastery of time helps the team master it, too. Strong leaders like Brady develop consistent processes they can apply to any project, teach their team to use them, and move their team towards a common goal.

If Brady's commitment to the team seems a bit extreme, that's because it is. There are personal costs to his level of devotion, and Brady regularly mentions that he misses out on certain elements of family life. His disciplined regimen (see Chapter 1) probably helps because his family knows when to expect him, and he can be fully engaged while they're together. Still, not every leader can sacrifice parts of their personal life for the team. To make it all work, the best leaders apportion their time with intent so they can put the time where it's needed most. They do whatever is needed to maintain their best performance and demonstrate how their teammates should spend their time.

ACTION FROM THE BUSINESS STADIUM: CARVING OUT THE TIME TO PREPARE

Nonprofit leaders face many of the same challenges as leaders in traditional business. Emma was the newly appointed CEO of a nonprofit for disadvantaged children from the inner city.

After years in investment banking, Emma was looking for a way to use her skills to improve the lives of others, and when this nonprofit opportunity came along, she jumped at the chance. But in her first several months on the job, she discovered a disappointing reality: the organization was struggling to meet the needs of the children it was serving. It wasn't due to typical nonprofit woes such as a shortage of money or volunteers; the children simply were not achieving the outcomes the organization strived for. It seemed like no matter what the staff did to motivate them, kids kept not showing up, risked failing out of school, or got into trouble with the law.

To understand the problem, Emma scheduled a meeting with David, a senior executive who had been with the organization since its inception several years before.

"David, I just don't get it," Emma began. "We have plenty of money and a capable, motivated staff. Our volunteers are terrific. We have all kinds of resources available for these children. So why aren't our kids finding more success?"

"I know," David sighed. "It's hugely frustrating. When we started, it was like nothing could stop us. But slowly, reality started to catch up to us, and we never really handled it well. In my opinion, our previous CEOs had tons of passion and energy, but just weren't up to the task of running an organization. They wanted so badly to help, but they didn't really know how to go about it. They needed to be running the organization like a business, but they couldn't get out of that 'task-completion' mindset."

"I know what you mean," Emma replied. "People forget that nonprofits are just like businesses. The goals may be different, but ultimately they need to be run like any other for-profit company. So let's talk specifics. What levers weren't the former CEOs pulling? What is missing?"

"In a way, I think we've lost focus on our mission," David lamented. "Not that we aren't trying to achieve what we've always wanted for the children. But more that we seem to have gotten so caught up in the day-to-day that we forget how it all ties into the greater goal. We've forgotten how little things are supposed to add up to help the big thing move forward.

"Here's an example from last year," David offered. "One staff member got a little behind on paperwork. He designed an after-school program that was really successful, and with the chaos of success, he didn't file some documents. He'd actually come in under budget, and the paperwork was just to release the excess funding. Understandably, he assumed it was no big deal. It was basically free money, so a slight delay in paperwork didn't matter, right? Besides, what he was working on instead was time-sensitive and needed to get done in order to keep his program successful. But what he didn't realize was that the money he held up in paperwork meant a delay in funding for an emergency relief program we started after that bad flood in town. He didn't mean to cause any harm; he just forgot that when all these little mechanisms don't turn, the bigger machine can't move."

"I get it," nodded Emma. "People need to keep the big picture in mind. You know, the organization does have well thought-out core values and a solid mission statement. And I've found documentation that at least one prior CEO tried to institute an annual action plan for the senior executives. Do you remember that?"

"Honestly, I forgot we ever wrote that mission statement and selected core values," David admitted. "And I don't remember anything about an action plan."

Emma now had an idea of how she could get the organization back on track. In her years in the business world, she came to understand how critical it was to have everyone, from leadership to the newest hire, on the same page. Just as Brady encouraged his teammates, Emma knew every staff member needed to be working towards the same goal in the same way. Like any business or sports team, this nonprofit needed to implement a system to ensure common understanding of that vision. Emma immediately went to work organizing a series of meetings to reintroduce the team to the organization's core values and mission, and to get them aligned towards the same specific goals.

Over the next several months, Emma and the executive team refined the organization's core values, updated the mission statement, and determined specific goals for the next ten-, five-, three-, and one-year periods. Once they decided on the one-year goals, they figured out the exact process to get there. As Brady had first done in high school, the team identified, step by step, what needed to be done and what milestones would mark their progress. They were particularly careful to include the children's outcomes in their measurement of success. In fact, those who write down goals are 33 percent more likely to achieve them.[10]

Once the strategic plan was in place, all the executives took the company-wide plan to their divisions and shared it with their teams. The response was very positive. Employees felt united in working towards the same goal. Each one understood better how their roles, large and small, contributed to the broader goals of the organization. Like Brady, many of them reprioritized their day-to-day tasks to better reflect what was actually most important, rather than just what was most time-sensitive.

Over the next year, Emma saw a real transformation take place within the organization. Operationally, meetings became more useful, processes ran more smoothly, and miscommunications practically disappeared. Staff morale experienced a huge boost. Most important of all, the children the organization served started achieving better results. Participation hit an all-time high, average grades improved, and instances of legal trouble decreased. By reminding employees what was most important and aligning them around a clearly defined common goal, the organization became more efficient and started making a real, lasting impact in the community.

GAME REVIEW:

- In every type of organization, leaders need a clear vision of the future and a precise plan to get there. Each member of the team needs to understand their role in the process, and why that contribution matters.
- Small problems often lead to bigger ones down the road. Develop a strategy to maintain high-quality, accurate work that completes the necessary tasks and moves the organization down the desired path.

EXECUTING THE PLAY

Exercises for the Preseason:

- Examine your daily schedule. Do you have a set routine? Does it prioritize what matters most? How do you manage challenges that arise unexpectedly?
- How much time are you able to invest in your team? Do they get shortchanged because you struggle to stay on top of your responsibilities? What is your team unable to do because you've been unable to make the time?
- Review your organization's core values, mission statement, and core purpose. Are they still accurate and up to date? Do they reflect the ultimate goal for which the organization is striving? Is everyone on the team aware of and aligned behind them?

Best Practices for the Game:

- Write your team's short- and long-term goals, including the step-by-step plan to get there, and post them in a high-traffic area. Visually track your team's progress towards taking each step. These visual representations will remind team members of the ultimate goal, and reinforce the importance of each person's contributions to the organization.

- Meet with each member of your team and examine their daily routines. Use your schedule as an example, and help them optimize their routine similarly. Have them evaluate whether each step moves the team closer to its goals and reflects what is most important. (Before you have this meeting, make sure you've done the same evaluation of your own routines!)

CHAPTER 3

Lead Through Each and Every Moment

"There was a lot of shit that happened tonight."[1]
—Tom Brady, after Super Bowl LI

A STEP-BY-STEP MIRACLE

It was a total disaster. A complete breakdown. Plenty thought the Atlanta Falcons would beat the New England Patriots in Super Bowl LI. After all, the Falcons had an amazing season. Head coach Dan Quinn was a highly respected defensive expert, who famously led the devastating "Legion of Boom" defense in Seattle. Offensive coordinator Kyle Shanahan was son of legendary coach Mike Shanahan, and proved to be an offensive savant in his own right. Always terrific quarterback Matt Ryan had a career year, throwing more than 4,900 yards and 38 touchdowns to only seven interceptions,[2] and winning NFL MVP.[3] The Falcons had the number one offense in the league, and they routed the Seattle Seahawks and Green Bay Packers in the playoffs on their way to the Super Bowl. So it was not shocking that the Falcons were beating the Patriots.

It was shocking how *badly* the Falcons were beating the Patriots.

After a scoreless first quarter, the game took a dramatic turn. Just a few seconds into the second quarter, Atlanta recovered a New England fumble, which the Falcons then turned into a touchdown. On their next possession, the Patriots had to punt the ball away, and again, the Falcons responded with a touchdown. The Patriots showed some life in their next possession, holding the ball for over six minutes and earning five first downs. But then, just outside the red zone, Tom Brady did the unthinkable: he threw an interception that the Falcons returned 82 yards for a touchdown.[4]

Brady rarely makes mistakes, and practically never throws interceptions. He's a top-five all-time leader in interception percentage, at a ridiculous 1.8 percent.[5] He's also been incredibly good at avoiding interceptions returned for touchdowns, called pick-sixes. Brady is also a top-five all-time leader in pass attempts, but each one of the other quarterbacks in that group has thrown for more than double the number of pick-sixes Brady has.[6] Brady has a remarkable record of sustained success, which made this Super Bowl pick-six all the more shocking.

The Patriots did get the ball once more before the end of the second quarter, but all they could manage was a measly three points from a field goal. Going into halftime, the Patriots were losing, 21–3.[7] No team had ever come back to win a Super Bowl if they were down by more than ten points.[8] And unbelievably, it got worse for the Patriots.

About halfway through the third quarter, the Falcons scored yet another touchdown.[9] The score was 28–3. The Patriots were down by 25 points, with barely one and a half quarters left to play. For most people, the game was essentially over. Brady has led more than his fair share of fourth-quarter comebacks,[10] but surely this deficit, with so little time remaining, was impossible even for him to overcome. It was an unbelievable situation. The country watched with jaws agape. The Patriots weren't just losing. They were getting destroyed. Embarrassed! The Falcons were unstoppable world-beaters, and the Patriots their pathetic victims. It was unlike anything the public had ever witnessed with the Brady-Bill Belichick Patriots.

And then Tom Brady went to work.

He picked his way down the field using a combination of short, quick passes and a strong running game. Brady even scrambled for 15 yards himself![11] On the thirteenth play of the drive, with just over two minutes left in the third quarter, Brady threw a touchdown pass. The kick for the extra point failed, but at least the Patriots got some points. New England's defense held Atlanta to a three-and-out, and as the fourth quarter began, the Falcons punted. Again Brady slowly progressed down the field, leading them far enough for a field goal. The score was 28–12 with less than ten minutes remaining.

Then the tide began to turn. Matt Ryan took a sack and fumbled, and New England recovered. Brady got sacked on first down, but continued down the field for a touchdown and two-point conversion. Suddenly the score was 28–20, with just under six minutes remaining. The Patriots edged closer.

After the Patriots' defense again forced the Falcons to punt, Brady got the ball back with three and a half minutes left in the game. If he could lead his team down the field one more time and execute another two-point conversion, the game would be, unbelievably, tied. And so Brady went to work again. Pass after pass, he marched his team down the field. They scored a touchdown and converted the two-point play. With less than a minute left, the score was tied at 28. The Falcons' offense couldn't produce anything in the final minute, and the last Patriots play of regulation only amounted to a few yards.[12] For the first time in NFL history, the Super Bowl went into overtime.[13]

In overtime, if the team that starts on offense scores a field goal, the other team gets a possession. However, if the team that starts on offense scores a touchdown, the game is over. As luck would have it, the Patriots won the coin toss.[14] So Tom Brady, who had just led his team to an incredibly unlikely comeback from 25 points down, put on his helmet to lead the charge downfield one final time.

Brady executed the same way he had on previous drives, the same way he did all season. Starting from the shotgun, Brady completed a series of short, quick passes and timely rushes to gain yards. Four minutes later, the Patriots were in the red zone and scored, ending the game with a sudden-death touchdown. The Patriots beat the Falcons, 34–28, to seize the Super Bowl.[15]

It was a momentous achievement. To most people watching, the game was over at halftime. Most of the third quarter was simply to put the nail in the Patriots' coffin. The Falcons absolutely dismantled the Patriots—until Brady led the team to 31 unanswered points and the victory.

Brady was ruthless, and ruthlessly efficient. At halftime, Brady and the team were calm, refusing to panic despite a disastrous first half.[16] Even when the Patriots were down by 25 points late in the third quarter, Brady reminded his team the game was not over.

Above all, Brady stuck to the game plan. He understood time was short, so he moved quickly, but did not rush. He used the same short, quick passes that brought so much success in the past. He allowed the running backs to do their jobs. Brady managed his team masterfully. Patriot Duron Harmon said after the game, "He led that team down there that whole fourth quarter, man. That's the Tom Brady quarter, man. Tom Brady quarter: That's what we're going to call it from now on."[17]

LEADERSHIP LESSONS FROM THE FIELD:

- Leaders cannot panic when time gets tight. The team will follow the emotions of the leader, and panic creates chaos, which wastes more time. The best leaders maintain calm in every situation, helping their team do the same. Cooler heads are more likely to prevail.
- When faced with a difficult situation, stick to the plan you designed with your team. Keep doing what made you successful in the past. Strong leaders let their team's excellent preparation guide them through challenges.

TIME MANAGEMENT IN THE MOMENT

When the rubber meets the road, it's difficult to keep a team intact and focused. Despite the best-laid plans, reality can break a scheme quickly and devastatingly. That's why exhaustive preparation is so key: in difficult situations, leaders need to depend on the team's prior practice to help them keep the team together, working towards the ultimate goal.

This is time management when it matters most. The leader first sets the tone by managing their own time so carefully and designing a playbook that works. The leader then helps the team do the same by helping them implement a similar playbook and preparing extensively to meet the challenges that could arise. And when it comes time to perform, the leader helps the team stay focused and rely on its training in order to weather the storm. Preparation helps the leader and teammates stay calm, a critical factor since stress negatively impacts brain performance[18] and impairs strategic thinking.[19] The team that can execute its carefully designed plan is more likely to succeed.

By keeping the team on task and working as planned, the leader still has the flexibility to respond to new crises and make adjustments as necessary. In Super Bowl LI, Brady kept his team calm and focused despite overwhelming odds. He led his teammates step by step through their regular routine. They stuck to what they practiced for and brought success in the past. Brady stayed mostly in the shotgun. He went through his pre-snap analysis of the defense and called out important information to his team. He tried to avoid pressure with short, quick passes to his receivers. He relied on teammates down the field to make effective blocks. When appropriate, he deferred to the running game and leaned on his backs to collect yardage. Brady's play that night was a master class in management.

Like the best business leaders, Brady knows the best way to efficiency is through either experience or practice. Repeatedly doing the same thing makes it part of a person's muscle memory and helps them perform it almost unconsciously. Reflexes are faster than conscious thought. By ensuring his team was thoroughly prepared, Brady had confidence his team could function despite a history-making deficit. Brady should be an example to business leaders everywhere. If you set an elite example and help your teammates prepare, your team can shine in even the unlikeliest moments.

ACTION FROM THE BUSINESS STADIUM: TOWN HALL TURMOIL

Theresa worked at a rapidly growing staffing firm. She was a young professional in the operations division and showed a lot of promise. Management was implementing a plan to strengthen and improve culture as the company continued to expand and open remote locations. An important part of the effort included regular company-wide town hall meetings that would introduce new initiatives, disseminate best practices, build community, and keep the whole company aligned. Everyone would attend the event in person, including colleagues from distant remote offices. All the senior executives would speak. Pulling it off would require considerable effort.

Impressed by Theresa's work so far with the new culture initiative and excited by her potential, the vice president of operations, Cara, asked Theresa to spearhead the town hall effort. It was like the skill Belichick initially identified in Brady. Theresa had no experience with large public events of this scale, but she was flattered to be chosen and ready to learn. Theresa was honest with Cara about her concerns, but accepted the responsibility and went right to work.

Theresa understood the first town hall was critically important. Leadership would introduce revamped core values, a new internal communications program, and a career development curriculum. Plus, the first meeting had to be engaging, or no one would want to return for the next one. This was the first introduction most of her colleagues would have to the new culture program, so the logistics and content of the meeting had to match the quality of the new program.

The first step was to brainstorm. Theresa had to take stock of everything she knew about public presentations, large-scale events, auditorium logistics, catering, performance, and more. She also had to identify everything she *didn't* know, so she could do research and seek assistance where necessary. Thankfully, Theresa had several months to plan, so she felt comfortable there would be plenty of time. Of course, part of the challenge for Theresa was that, not having done this before, she didn't know what she didn't know.

Theresa started plugging away. She gathered a team, and together they began planning. They had some great ideas to make the event fun and even a little surprising. They started to consider who would MC the event, which executives would speak about each topic, and whether they should hire outside resources. They explored the idea of getting some indoor special effects to wow the crowd. After all, every football team has some trick plays up its sleeve!

Still, Theresa started to have reservations about her team's progress. They were ready to make a couple big splashes, but on the day of the meeting, they would still have to advance the program enough to *get to* the splashes. It was as if Brady and his teammates were going through the motions at practice, but not actually getting any better. Theresa felt like a lot of logistics had been discussed, but not actually enacted. She sought advice from Cara.

"Cara, I'm beginning to worry about the town hall. I'm not sure we've made enough progress, and I'm starting to fear we won't be able to get it all done in time," Theresa confessed.

"OK," said Cara slowly, taking in the information. "Tell me where you are right now."

Cara listened as Theresa broke down the structure of the event, described the basic logistics, shared the list of topics and speakers, and explained some of the fun elements planned. Cara was happy about the good ideas Theresa and her team had, but grew increasingly concerned about the coordination to make it all happen.

"Let me tell you what I'm hearing," responded Cara. "You have a nice overall design and some good concepts for how the town hall will work. But you haven't told me one thing about the details that will make it all function on the big day. I think you need to take a step back and look at the basics. Are you actually ready to open the auditorium doors on the big day? All the funny jokes and charming presentation elements won't mean anything if you haven't, say, set up a sound system for the audience to hear them. Even before that, do you have a script?"

Theresa was crestfallen. She knew Cara was right—they were still basically on step one. Even the most fundamental logistics weren't in place.

"And another thing," Cara continued. "You need to start problem solving *now*. However well you plan, something *will* go wrong. It might not be your fault, but you need to be prepared for it."

Theresa left the meeting sobered but focused. She had a much better grasp on what she needed to do. More importantly, she understood this project was much bigger than she could accomplish alone. She needed each member of the team to contribute at the highest level.

Theresa gathered her team and explained their new plan was to start from the bottom up. They could worry about pizzazz later—first they needed to ensure a clean, organized, well-planned event. Theresa and her team scrapped their old plans and worked the logistics of the town hall step by painstaking step. Theresa consulted outside experts and brought back insights to the team. She then used the collective brainpower of the team to surface every possible detail, process, and hazard.

When remote employees arrived on campus, where would they go? They needed signs directing people to a central gathering place, where there should probably be coffee and other refreshments available. That would require a table and tablecloth. Was there an outlet in an appropriate place? How would they tell people the event was starting and they needed to take their seats? Were there enough seats in the auditorium? What would the audience see on stage as they walked in? Did they know how to turn the lights on? How many microphones would they need, including handheld and clip-on? What time did presenters need to arrive in order to ensure they would be ready to go on stage? Did the podium need to be on wheels? Would there be chairs on stage? Theresa knew some presenters preferred PowerPoint, while others liked Prezi. Could they accommodate different formats? What if a presenter wanted to make a last-minute change to a speech?

The team broke down every single element of the presentation, and the list went on and on. Like Brady, Theresa developed a detailed playbook that accounted for every step in the process and had buy-in from the whole team. It was a draining process, but Theresa finally felt they had a good path to success. Over the next two months, Theresa and her team worked tirelessly, creating a detailed plan for the day, anticipating problems that could arise, and negotiating with vendors. She saw the progress they were making, but her stress level still rose as the town hall date crept ever closer. Cara saw Theresa's anxiety grow and called her into her office.

"You've been giving me weekly updates, I've sat in on a few of your meetings, and I've signed vendor contracts. You're making real progress towards this town hall. But you look like you're coiled tighter than a spring," said Cara. "Tell me what's going on."

Theresa took a deep breath in. Forget Brady—Theresa felt like *she* was the one down by 25 points late in the third quarter.

"I. Am. Freaking. Out." she began, putting her hand to her forehead. "I'm afraid we're about to spin out of control. We've come so far, but there's still *so much* to do, and we only have a couple weeks left. I'm losing faith I can actually do it.

"I feel like it's all about to fall apart. Several speakers missed deadlines to submit their speeches and slide decks. I ordered these special coins for attendees to take home and remind them of our core values, but the factory in China just told me they shut down for Chinese New Year and now won't be able to deliver in time. I still have to finalize the menus. I don't know how I'm going to do it all."

"Theresa, listen to me very carefully," Cara insisted. "I am not going to let you fail. Stop even imagining it because it's not an option.

"Now, I've seen your event binder. Everyone on your team has one. You're communicating well and everyone understands what the next step is, right?" When Theresa nodded, Cara continued, "Then you need to trust the plan. That's why you went through the whole process of breaking the event down into such minute detail—so you and your team could design a plan that included everything necessary. You mapped a path to success. Now go follow it.

"You also mentioned all these things you're personally doing. But remember, you have a whole team, and you just confirmed to me they're capable and understand what needs to be done. Are you really leveraging their abilities? It's awfully hard to lead a team if you don't rely on your teammates.

"Lead your team by example, and have faith in the plan. You take care of your responsibilities, and let your teammates do the jobs they were assigned, the jobs they agreed to do. Stay calm. Your team will reflect your attitude."

Suddenly, it clicked for Theresa. All the preparation she and her team did was for this very moment. When Brady finds his team down late in the game, he does not panic. He reminds them of their game plan and tells them to execute just as they practiced. Theresa collected herself, reviewed her event binder, and meticulously worked her way through her tasks one by one. She regularly checked in with her teammates to make sure they stayed on track, but let them do their jobs without interference.

Like Brady, Theresa led her team by example. She managed her time carefully and completed every responsibility she had. She followed the team's plan to the letter and helped her teammates do the same. If a presenter missed a deadline, she found out how she or her team could help finish the job. She organized two full dress rehearsals to prepare the presenters and work out all the kinks. As the countdown to the town hall approached, Theresa and her team were functioning crisply and well on their way to a successful event.

On the day of the event, several issues arose, but like Brady and his team, Theresa and her team overcame them with their careful planning. When one speaker went long, Theresa had the MC seamlessly shorten a transition just as they planned in case of a time issue. When a microphone went out, one of Theresa's teammates immediately replaced it with the backup he had at the ready. The town hall was a huge success. The employees were excited about the new core values and culture program, and the remote offices started to feel more connected to the rest of the company.

Cara was thrilled with Theresa's performance and couldn't wait for the next town hall. Theresa learned from all the missteps and successes of the first meeting and refined the preparation process. She learned to rely on her team and trust the plan. Theresa continued her success, and both she and the company grew better.

GAME REVIEW:

- Even if there's no opportunity to practice the plan before you must execute, just the act of creating a plan and developing team buy-in can help drive success. As the process gets underway, team members will still understand expectations, know their next steps, and feel confident about where to turn if there's a problem.
- Leading a team to victory is just that—leading a TEAM. You have to use the skills of the people involved to gain the collective and exponential benefit.
- Strong leadership skills are necessary in every layer of a company. Even the lowest-level employee can demonstrate excellent leadership from within the

(Continued on next page)

team and help the group succeed. In fact, the best leaders are great at encouraging intra-team leadership.
- The plan you develop with your team needs to be thorough and include contingencies. Anticipate what could go wrong, and develop responses now. When it's time to put the plan into action, have your preprepared solutions at the ready. When things go wrong, your team will both know what to do and have the resources in place to keep the plan on track.

EXECUTING THE PLAY

Exercises for the Preseason:
- Consider the leadership role you play within your own team. If you are a designated leader, how do you encourage team members to display their own leadership? If you are a rank-and-rile member, how do you demonstrate your own leadership capabilities? In either case, what can you do to improve?
- The next time something goes wrong, evaluate your reaction. Do you immediately panic? Do you overthink and hesitate? Effective leaders emote calm energy that spreads to the team and keeps them focused.

Best Practices for the Game:
- Gather your team and review your standard operating procedures or playbook. Brainstorm things that could go wrong, and determine solutions. Then work as a team to incorporate that problem-solving into the preparatory work you would do for any project. Make sure everyone has a role and can fill it with confidence.
- Similarly, gather your team for a postmortem after your next project. What went well, and what didn't? How can you avoid the same problems in the future? Make sure you do this as soon as possible after you complete the project, when memories are freshest.

PART II
Prepping for Game Time

CHAPTER 4

Meetings Are a Championship Tool

"We've been at it a long time, so there's a lot of consistency."[1]
—Tom Brady, on his film sessions with Bill Belichick

BRADY TRANSFORMS MEETINGS INTO TEAM-BUILDING OPPORTUNITIES

Imagine this situation: you are an offensive lineman in the NFL. You're not a star, but you're a solid player with a strong performance history in the NFL. You're in your first season with the Tampa Bay Buccaneers, and your third team overall. During a lifetime in football, from Pee Wee to high school to college and the pros, you've lost plenty of games. The experience still doesn't make it any easier.

It's the third game of the regular season and the Buccaneers are losing, badly. The team is having problems everywhere. On one play, your defense had a complete coverage breakdown that led to the opponent scoring a touchdown. A special teams player on the other team made a spectacular play and blocked one of your field-goal attempts. On offense, in one moment, the referees missed an incredibly obvious penalty that should have resulted in a Bucs first down. In the next moment, one of your receivers dropped a pass that bounced off his hands. On another play, a different receiver stopped running his route before the play was over, only to discover that if he had kept going, he would have been all alone with a clear path to the end zone. On a critical third down, your tight end whiffed on a key block that allowed Brady to get sacked. Nearly everything that could have gone wrong, has gone wrong.

It's midway through the third quarter, so there's still a bit of time left in the game. But if the Bucs are going to get some momentum going, the team needs to start playing better *now*. You see your quarterback, Tom Brady, on the bench talking to the offensive coordinator. They're deep in discussion, and it doesn't look like a cheerful conversation. Brady seems more animated than usual while studying the prior plays on the sideline tablet computer.

Suddenly, Brady is up, stalking the sidelines. He corrals his linemen, including you, and his receivers and backs, and gathers everyone together on a bench. You're all sitting while he's standing in front of you. He begins to turn red in the face, and his scowl looks intimidating. Once he knows he has everyone's attention, he lets loose. He yells, demanding attention to detail and smart decisions. He screams about the need for explosive speed and sharp cuts. You haven't been playing with him long, but you've never seen Brady like this before. You recoil.

After this outburst, it's clear that everything you've heard about Brady's sideline alter ego, "Psycho Tom," is true. On game day, Brady, when mad, displays a whole different side to his personality. There's something wild in his eyes as he rips into his offense. Energy radiates from his whole body.

Yet you notice that for a guy who is enraged and yelling, he's also oddly composed. Admittedly, his tone and volume make him sound angry and maybe a little untamed, but his words aren't actually abusive. Instead, they clearly lay out what he needs from the offense in order to succeed. He makes demands, but doesn't insult anyone. It's hard not to be taken by Brady's passion. He wants, no, *needs*, this win badly and will do whatever it takes to get it. He will push himself and his teammates to the limit to seize the win.

Indeed, the offense does improve somewhat after Brady's fiery delivery. You all don't play spectacularly, but at least it's mistake-free football. Despite the improvement, the score remains lopsided, but at least it's no longer embarrassing. Still, with four minutes left in the fourth quarter, you know it's over. Dejected fans start to leave Raymond James Stadium, home of the Buccaneers. Brady sits on a bench, looking too disgusted to speak. He exudes silent fury. No one dares go near him.

Mercifully, the game ends. The locker room is quiet. Guys go about their business so they can get home as soon as possible. As you drive home, your thoughts turn to the team's next practice. It's going to be miserable. You've been with two other NFL teams, and those practice facilities were always uncomfortable places after a loss. Coaches were angry with themselves for their poor planning and angry with players for their missed execution. Film sessions felt interminable, and everyone was publicly shamed for his mistakes. Players criticized each other and sometimes tried to deflect blame. The experience was always profoundly disheartening.

What will happen in the practice facility strikes anxiety into your brain. You've heard rumors of Bill Belichick's notoriously harsh film sessions, and after 20 years together, it's safe to assume Brady adopted his former coach's routine. Brady is going to light into everyone during the offensive unit film session. If he was angry during his sideline speech, no doubt he'll be even angrier after stewing on the loss for 24 hours. It's going to be a very long day.

You wake up in the morning dreading the day to come. You don't think you made any serious errors during the game, but you're sure something you did will be exposed on film in front of the whole team. You're not sure if Brady is going to yell with rage or growl with contempt, but you are sure it's going to be very unpleasant.

Entering the practice facility, you find your way to the offense's meeting room and select a seat in the middle of a crowd. You intentionally wear a shirt the same color as the chairs. From prior experience, you know that blending in is key: be invisible and don't draw any attention to yourself. You may be pointed out on film for screwing up, but there's no need to remind the quarterback you're there and potentially make it worse. You open your notebook and brace for the beatdown.

Brady walks in. He turns on the equipment. You cringe in anticipation of his rage. But then . . . nothing. Brady doesn't open the meeting with a yell. He doesn't inform the team exactly how terribly they played. He doesn't shame them for mistakes or cringe in disgust.

Instead, Brady speaks calmly. He's going through the film and analyzing the Xs and Os, but he's not cruel, or rude, or even angry. In fact, he's not raising his voice at all. He seems far more like a professor than the fierce competitor you know him to be. *What is happening?* You are absolutely stunned.

You sit in shock for a moment, but quickly realize you're missing what Brady is saying. He's giving a thorough assessment of the offense's play. He points out individual mistakes, but there are no accusations or vitriol to accompany it. He asks questions about why guys made certain decisions, but he's not looking for a "gotcha!" moment. Instead, he really listens to what they say and tries to understand their thinking so he can explain how to reach a better decision next time. He makes suggestions on how to recognize a certain type of defensive coverage and on what players should do when they spot it. As he discusses plays with his teammates, he calls them "babe," and other affectionate nicknames.

You're absorbed by his analysis, by his creative problem solving and clarity of vision. He's really an excellent teacher. You're learning a great deal in this film session and getting good advice on how to improve your play. Even though Brady shows two mistakes you made, you actually feel more confident now than you did before. He asks some pointed questions of various players, but never puts anyone on the spot or embarrasses them.[2] There is some friendly razzing from Brady and others, but it's not mean-spirited; it lightens the mood and makes everyone laugh.

Before you even realize, the meeting is over. Somehow, it's been an almost pleasant experience. The session not only helped the team improve its strategy, but also brought the team closer together. You've never been in a film session like this, where players learn exactly what they did wrong, but feel better prepared for the next time instead of terrified of making the same mistake again. The offense understands exactly what they need to work on this week. It's hard to believe, but you're almost looking forward to the next offensive unit film session.

You spend the rest of the day thinking about your experience that morning. In one meeting, you've developed a whole new respect for Tom Brady. He covered all the same material that any other coach or quarterback would, but he did it in a way that was constructive rather than demeaning. In hindsight, his anger on the sideline even makes more sense. Brady understands that the game is a time for fiery speeches and emotion. But he also understands that meetings are a time for digesting and learning. From the way teammates answered questions, it was obvious they were working to see things the way Brady sees them. By the end of the season, you will be almost perfectly in sync and able to handle any game situation. It might not come right away, but these useful, engaging film sessions will move the team towards that goal one meeting at a time.

LEADERSHIP LESSONS FROM THE FIELD:

- Meetings are opportunities to discuss problems and exchange ideas on how to solve them. Leaders who listen will understand their team and be better able to put them on the right path.
- It's OK to show emotion, and in fact can be useful. But make sure the time and place are appropriate for the emotion you're displaying.

(Continued on next page)

- Belittling people will not generate the improved performance you are after. Speak to your colleagues with intention, but give feedback that is constructive rather than mean-spirited.

WHY MEETINGS MATTER

This story says a great deal about the purpose and tone of effective meetings. It doesn't get into the specifics of their meeting structure or the content they covered. What is clear is that the meeting is highly organized. Brady takes the team through a detailed analysis of the game, asks questions, and elicits feedback. Brady, as the leader and facilitator, keeps the meeting focused, covers all necessary topics, and engages each attendee. The meetings achieve the analysis, debate, alignment, and team building he is seeking. He makes the time together both pleasant and useful, strengthening team cohesion and personal relationships. Brady explains, "My leadership is more about connecting with someone instead of calling him out in front of my teammates."[3] The lineman leaves looking forward to the next meeting, a rarity in team sports and in business.

If you're like most people, you dread meetings. And really, who can blame you? It's tough to have a positive attitude about a mandatory activity that often goes on too long, is wretchedly boring, gets dominated by a few loud voices, and accomplishes little or nothing. Studies show that bad meeting practices correlate with lower levels of market share, less innovation, increased turnover, and decreased job satisfaction.[4] No wonder people find any excuse to avoid meetings. You just don't get paid enough for that kind of torture.

Regular, standardized meetings build a structured routine that allow people to unearth problems before they happen, or at least to get ahead of them before it's too late. In the film session, Brady not only identifies trouble, but also teaches his team how to avoid making the same mistake. Reactive business administration is likely to fail. When unexpected challenges arise, it's nearly impossible to keep everything in order if there isn't already practiced procedure in place to keep the ship afloat while you repair the leak. Chaos naturally takes over, and the impact is staggering: in 2019, poorly run meetings cost US companies nearly $400 billion.[5]

It's no accident the subtitle to Patrick Lencioni's classic book *Death by Meeting* is *"A Leadership Fable."*[6] One of the most crucial skills in any leader's tool chest is the ability to hold great meetings. Leaders set the standard across the company, so when they prepare, organize, and facilitate great meetings, others are more likely to do the same.

Just like Brady's film session, well-run meetings create alignment among teams and allow attendees to solve issues more quickly. While bad meetings can feel interminable, good meetings actually save everyone time and make companies more efficient. Effective meetings also encourage good communication skills, which is often the biggest problem companies face.[7]

Meetings without goals and structure waste time, not only for the attendees, but also for any non-attendees who could otherwise be tapping into the knowledge of those in the meeting. Poor meetings often cause employee disengagement and a lack of clarity around a company's vision. Plus, they're disheartening and can make employees resentful. A whopping 71 percent of senior managers across industries said meetings are unproductive and inefficient.[8] You'd be surprised at how quickly terrible meetings can erode culture and morale.

The number one key to preparing well-led meetings is having the right people in the meeting. Attendees should consist of a manageable number who have a legitimate purpose for being there and who can filter down critical information from one level to the next.

Once you know the *who*, it's about the *when*. Preparing effective meetings should take into account appropriate scheduling. In his bestselling book *Scaling Up*,[9] Verne Harnish encourages daily, weekly, monthly, quarterly, and annual meetings that keep people aligned and working towards the same vision. These meetings need to get on everyone's calendars as soon as they're scheduled. Quarterly and annual meetings in particular should be calendared at least a year in advance. Nothing should get in the way of these critical events. According to Harnish, daily, weekly, and monthly meetings should be so routine that people know when they are before they even make it onto the calendar.

Still, as Brady knows, having the right people in the room at the right time doesn't guarantee championship meeting results. You need to master organization with good meeting structures. The use of best practices from resources such as *Scaling Up* or The Entrepreneurial Operating System®[10] will help you create highly organized systems and processes for achieving specific meeting goals and maximizing everyone's time and contribution. In a daily huddle, for example, many business coaches suggest attendees stand for the whole ten or so minutes to encourage brevity and speed. The meeting script should be designed to permit answers of 15 words or fewer from each attendee. The point is to share daily priorities, update scheduling, and get everyone on the same page. A brief, no-chairs meeting is a great vehicle to achieve that daily goal.

Like Brady, the best leaders understand it's critical to foster well-facilitated meetings. Even with well-planned meetings, facilitation can make the time more useful and productive. Brady's give and take with his offensive unit is one example of good meeting facilitation. Now, the boss or team leader doesn't have to lead the meeting him or herself. In fact, one of the best ways to ensure well-run meetings is to inspire everyone to sharpen their facilitation skills by rotating the duty.

Great leaders are good *attendees* of meetings, too (even Brady is a good attendee—see Chapter 11). Like any other attendee, leaders should prepare for each meeting carefully, reviewing relevant materials and bringing necessary documents. They must show up on time, focus on the task at hand, and contribute willingly but without dominating the conversation. In fact, to truly elevate other members of the team, leaders should share their own ideas last, not first, regardless of whether they're facilitating.

Many leaders choose to delegate facilitation duties to other attendees (or even to neutral third parties, like business coaches) who are particularly adept at leading meetings. Good facilitators obtain discussion items from participants and send an agenda in advance. They ensure that any resources or logistics required for the meeting are coordinated. Once the meeting begins, facilitators must keep attendees on topic and on time. Facilitators also need to spark conversation and debate, but without allowing the discussion to go down a rabbit hole or fixate on minutiae. They need to prevent the loudest voices from dominating the conversation or bending the will of the group. They need to engage every participant to elicit their ideas and feedback. This requires an understanding of the issues at hand, an awareness of the personalities involved, and the confidence to steer the participants, even if some of them outrank the facilitator.

Everything Brady does is designed with Super Bowls in mind. Similarly, design your meeting structures with your team's end goal in mind. Be disciplined, and periodically review the effectiveness of your meeting structures. All the little decisions made in meetings add up to determine whether your team is effectively working towards the ultimate goal—so bad meetings can lead to terrible consequences. With good structure, the content of the next meeting will flow naturally from the content of the last, just like a series of well-structured plays in a football game.

Structure gives you the rules of the game, but you still need the on-field performance of the meeting—the content. If all this preparation sounds like a lot of work, it is—just like a full week of practice before the game on Sunday. Larger, less frequent meetings in particular will require more work in advance. Incorporating these meetings into your regular routine will make them feel less burdensome. You'll develop a good rhythm in which ideas flow, collaboration blossoms, and important decisions get made wisely.

Practice will help you lock in meeting performance standards among the team. Once established, be careful not to let standards slip. Sloppiness in something as simple as attendance at a daily huddle can spread into other aspects of meetings. Once standards fall, people deemphasize the importance of consistency. Then you're in danger of a lackadaisical attitude seeping into other aspects of the business. To keep things fresh, divide up the meeting roles so no one person carries the entire burden. Switch off between facilitators (as long as they're trained), or assign a different person each week to send the meeting recap. This tactic has the added effect of making the whole team own the meeting, with each member invested in its success and in improving the skill set.

Now, just like a streak of Sunday wins, successful meetings can breed arrogance. Once meeting structures are firmly in place, some attendees may eventually come to feel that meetings are pointless because it seems like few serious problems are ever unearthed. Of course, that's the whole *point* of regular check-ins. Only steadily performed, productive meetings can avert problems and keep the business running smoothly. Brady lives this truth every week.

ACTION FROM THE BUSINESS STADIUM: BETTER MEETINGS PRODUCE BETTER PERFORMANCE

Mike, the CEO of an insurance company, had been holding separate weekly meetings with each person on his five-member executive team. They also had one weekly group meeting with the CEO, the five executives, and 12 senior managers.

Mike had good instincts, and given his inexperience as a leader, the meeting structure he designed wasn't terrible. Individual meetings ensured Mike got quality face time with each executive. It gave everyone a chance to review thoroughly what was happening in each division and dig deep into any problems. Mike and his executives always came well prepared, and their time together was prioritized so that other issues would not supersede the meetings. Much like Brady's offensive unit meetings, Mike's weekly group meetings with the executive team and senior managers were designed to ensure everyone was on the same page, even if they weren't always able to solve all the problems that surfaced in conversation. Things at the company were going OK. They were generally successful, although they sometimes struggled with execution—after all, even Brady throws the occasional interception. And there always seemed to be some drama within the executive team, with members getting snippy or passive aggressive with each other in their weekly team meetings. It was slightly annoying to many, but all in all, things weren't bad.

And just like Brady, Mike was convinced that good wasn't good enough. While meetings were mostly productive and useful, Mike felt a constant time crunch. He was always running up against strategic planning deadlines and falling behind on long-term projects because of his tight schedule. Mike had smart people working for him, and the industry was booming—so why wasn't his company doing better? He decided to hire Natalie, a respected business coach, to get to the root of the problem and improve everyone's performance.

Natalie spent some time interviewing the executives and sat in on a couple meetings. After her initial analysis, it was clear to Natalie what was happening.

She explained to Mike, "Your meeting structures are not completely effective. They're well intended—I know you're trying to develop strong relationships with your executives and to support them. But this individual meeting pattern is actually hurting all of you."

"How so?" Mike asked, surprised that something as seemingly inconsequential as his meeting schedule was the thing Natalie was emphasizing.

"Think about the math," Natalie suggested. "You have five executives each attending an individual one-hour meeting. Plus

I'm hearing they often go over their scheduled time from all the running around you do to solve the problems that come up during these one-on-one sessions. That's basically at least one whole day per week that you lose to meetings. No wonder you feel pressed for time," she assessed.

"And then there's the distraction factor," she added. "When you're really in a good work groove, isn't it awful being interrupted?"

Mike nodded firmly in agreement.

"So think about how your executives feel," Natalie said. "You often interrupt them to answer questions that arise in individual meetings with other executives. They feel like they can't get a moment of quiet concentration."

Mike tilted his head to the side, realizing the truth in Natalie's words.

"I've never thought of it that way," he confessed.

"There's another related problem, too," Natalie said. "The only time you and your executive team meet as a group is at a once-a-week meeting that also includes senior managers."

"Right," Mike hesitated, inquisitively.

"So you never actually have your five executives meeting with you as a team unit," Natalie explains. "The individual meetings may be useful, but the overall structure doesn't build the 'team' aspect of your 'executive team.' You function more as a communication hub than as the leader of a team.

"They'll never be a team if they're never together as an exclusive group," she continued. "If the executives can't communicate problems to each other in a safer space, they'll keep going at each other in front of the senior managers. If you present a disunited front to the senior managers, you can't expect the managers to return to their own teams with a confident message about the company's direction."

Mike was distraught. In his genuine desire to support his executives, had he really so thoroughly damaged the team and the company?

"Don't worry, Mike," Natalie encouraged, seeing the look on his face. "There's a relatively easy fix for this. You'll still get the face time you want, but your executives' working relationships will improve, and you'll all be more productive." Mike relaxed a bit.

Natalie went right to work correcting meeting routines. She had the company transition to a set meeting structure, with a regular routine of daily, weekly, monthly, quarterly, and annual meetings. Mike started having one 15-minute daily huddle with all five executives and kept the one weekly meeting with both executives and senior managers.

After implementing and adjusting to the new system, Mike and the executive team were amazed at how much better they functioned as a unit. Just like Brady's meeting with his offense, suddenly all five executives were getting the same message at the same time. Problems got tackled systematically, collaboratively, and immediately during the huddles rather than ad hoc during individual meetings.

In one case, a full-on IT disaster was averted when one executive clarified the repercussions of a step he was planning to take. The executives even started to get along better personally and really coalesced as a team. Mike saved more than four hours every week by ending his many long individual meetings. Further, weekly group meetings with executives and senior managers presented an executive team that was aligned and united, making the meetings more productive and useful for everyone.

The changes in meeting structures did require some getting used to by Mike and the executive team, but the transition wasn't complicated. Yet over the course of a year, these relatively simple changes made the company go from a modest success to a real star in the insurance industry. The company ran more smoothly, employees at every level were happier, and clients and partners noticed a marked difference in the quality of products and services they received. By examining the purpose of meetings, Mike was able to develop a meeting structure more like Brady's, and his company moved towards victory.

MORE ACTION FROM THE BUSINESS STADIUM: POOR MEETINGS REFLECT POOR LEADERSHIP

An IT managed services company learned the hard way the danger of meeting disintegration. Owners Liam, Mason, and Ben painstakingly built their company by incorporating a specific meeting structure. The three men had a daily huddle, and implemented quarterly, monthly, and weekly meetings with senior staff. Like Brady, the owners found a great deal of success by taking this approach. But they were growing unhappy with the daily huddle structure. As the company expanded, they managed growth, hired smart people, and invested in their team. Each owner managed a different division of the company, and there wasn't a ton of overlap they needed to discuss. They felt their daily huddle was becoming unnecessary, taking time and attention from more important objectives that could produce real opportunity for the company. The business was running smoothly and all indicators were strong. Like Brady, Liam, Mason, and Ben had carefully crafted a well-oiled machine. They felt there simply wasn't a need for an owner huddle every single day.

As a team, the owners agreed to reduce the number of huddles to three per week. At first, the new arrangement seemed to work. This new structure left them plenty of time to address all necessary big-picture items. They got used to the new huddle system and found it functioned well. They also noticed it didn't matter if one of them missed a huddle now and then. The other two would let the third know if anything important happened. Things otherwise continued on as they had been. Eventually, if Liam, Mason, or Ben couldn't make a huddle on a particular day, they would just cancel it for the day. A week here or there with only two huddles would be fine. The company was still running well enough that they could surely make up for a missed huddle during the next one.

For a while, things carried on as smoothly as before. But after a while, Liam, Mason, and Ben started noticing their weekly meetings with senior staff weren't as productive as before. Administrative issues started hijacking the meetings. Little operational problems started to get in the way of discussing strategic initiatives the three owners prioritized for these meetings. It was like a sloppy snap on the football field. It didn't cause the play to break down entirely, but it did require extra effort and quick thinking by the players to save it.

Liam, Mason, and Ben also noticed that attendance was starting to falter at these weekly meetings. It meant they couldn't always get information required for important decisions. Truancy was occasionally frustrating, but the owners chalked it up to company growth and extra work required of the team. They convinced themselves it was a good problem to have.

One day, Lily, the senior manager of the payroll department, approached Mason with unease.

"Mason," she began, "I've found some unusual patterns in our cash reserves. I don't want to be alarmist, but I do think it's a problem we may need to explore."

"OK," replied Mason carefully, "Tell me more."

"It seems we're starting to develop an issue with cash flow. It's not a crisis, but it has been slowly worsening for the last couple months. If it starts moving any faster, I'm worried the company eventually might have trouble meeting payroll," Lily admitted.

"And you haven't been able to find a reason for this change?" asked Mason. When Lily shook her head no, Mason replied, "OK. I'm going to bring this up with Liam and Ben at our next meeting and see if they can think of anything in their own departments that might be causing the problem. In the meantime, please keep a close eye on it, and let me know about any developments," he requested.

Mason mentioned this to Liam and Ben at their next huddle, but none of them knew offhand why this might be happening, especially since business seemed generally good. Unfortunately, they didn't have much time to discuss it because several new fires had ignited since their last huddle.

For the company's monthly and quarterly meetings, Liam, Mason, and Ben always brought in an outside facilitator, a longtime business consultant named Brian. Over the next few monthly meetings with senior staff, Brian noticed several patterns. Time was increasingly spent dealing with operational issues. Brian wasn't sure why, since these problems should have been surfaced and solved easily in daily huddles. Then during the quarterly meeting, so much time was spent resolving basic administrative problems that Brian barely had time to track the company's progress towards its annual goals. He also noticed that some tactical issues raised during previous monthly meetings came up again because they hadn't been solved.

Brian was perplexed. All the company's meetings seemed to be losing effectiveness. He was there to manage productive strategic meetings that moved the company tangibly closer to its annual goals and its Big Hairy Audacious Goal (BHAG®).[11] Instead, they were spending so much time firefighting that Brian was basically facilitating operational meetings. It didn't seem the business was in peril, but it was clear it was off the path to sustained growth.

Listening to the meeting conversations, Brian also picked up on some cash flow problems. Worse, Brian learned the company lost out on a few sizable opportunities because they couldn't get organized in time to meet proposal deadlines. It was as if a football team committed a silly penalty away from the ball that negated a huge gain by the running back. Never a problem for the company before, it had now happened more than once.

Concerned, Brian approached Liam, Mason, and Ben after the quarterly meeting. The owners acknowledged some falling productivity, and even a little unusual testiness among the three of them. They asked Brian to explore the cause. After an investigation, Brian unraveled the mess and got to the root of the problem. At a meeting with the three owners, Brian explained the situation.

"The cause of your troubles might be surprising to hear," Brian warned. "The problem started small and rather simply. You three had been doing well with your daily huddles. You had a good handle on what was happening in each division. Daily, you shared ideas and supported one another. You could tackle problems quickly as they arose and prevent them from becoming crises. In short, you were performing well as leaders."

Liam, Mason, and Ben were incredulous. Was Brian suggesting that their huddles were causing all of these problems? It seemed ridiculous.

"When you started to tire of the daily huddles and abandon the process, things slowly began to unravel," Brian continued. "As your daily huddles decreased, so did your understanding of the company's ongoing needs. You each lost your thorough awareness of what was happening around the company, which in turn meant you couldn't adjust your own divisions to meet company needs. Without daily meetings, the alignment among you three faltered, and you became frustrated with each other for not perceiving the subtleties you once did."

The three leaders looked skeptical, but Brian went on, undeterred.

"Weekly meetings with your senior team became less useful. The three of you had to spend more of that time catching up on getting aligned and handling administrative issues you hadn't resolved during huddles. This then impacted the monthly meetings, which in turn rendered the quarterly meetings practically useless," Brian finished.

"Brian, you can't be serious," responded an annoyed Liam. "You're suggesting profound damage from something so small, so insignificant. A few huddles? It can't be," he concluded.

"Unfortunately, I'm quite serious. I know it may sound minor, but small things build up quickly into considerable issues. You guys fell away from what made you successful in the first place. It's simply not sustainable," Brian said. Brian understood, like Brady, that long-term goals can't be achieved without getting the details right.

Brian went on, and it only got worse. Most troubling was his discovery that the cash flow issues were stemming from a six-month backlog in billing clients. Accounts payable was something the team usually covered in monthly meetings, but it kept getting pushed off the agenda by operational problems. It was only due to Lily's diligence that the problem even surfaced. This billing backlog would have been caught easily under the original meeting structure, and it probably wouldn't have taken more than a brief weekly meeting to resolve. But even if it had been caught, if Liam, Mason, and Ben weren't disciplined enough to attend daily huddles, they likely couldn't be counted on to attend issue-specific meetings, either. The modest daily huddle was, in fact, a key to their success, and they had abandoned it.

"Since you three as leaders deemphasized the discipline of your daily huddles, the rest of your employees got sloppy with their huddles as well. That's why everyone is spending more time firefighting than growing," asserted Brian. "One little thing snowballed, and you created an avalanche."

Dedication to a regular meeting structure is incredibly important to your team's ability to function at a basic level, and its ability to accomplish growth. Brian and Brady understand that without well-run meetings, a team cannot function as an effective unit. When employees—and especially leaders—fail to respect how critical meetings are to success, ripples become tsunamis. Urgent, time-sensitive issues come up and prevent leadership from dealing with the most important issues. Leaders like Brady who commit to organize, prepare, and facilitate great meetings are better able to build efficient teams with strong cultures and avoid problems. Make your meetings work for you, just as Brady has for his team.

GAME REVIEW:

- Well-organized and well-facilitated meetings can build team cohesion, just as poorly done meetings can destroy it.
- Don't neglect the humble daily huddle with your team. It may feel inconsequential, but it's absolutely critical to surfacing issues early and maintaining a smooth path to success.
- Don't assume the most *immediate* issues are the most *important* issues.
- Leaders set the standard for meetings. How they organize, facilitate, and attend meetings will carry through to every level of the company.

EXECUTING THE PLAY

Exercises for the Preseason:

- Help your team understand and take ownership of effective meetings. Seek out facilitation training, and read resources such as *Death by Meeting* by Patrick Lencioni.
- Agree on a regular meeting schedule with your team. The schedule should be entered in everyone's calendars at least a year in advance. This will help inform their decisions on long-term planning, such as setting production deadlines and taking vacations. Be sure to include the following meeting types:
  - Annual planning
  - Quarterly review
  - Monthly planning
  - Weekly tactical
  - Daily huddle

Best Practices for the Game:

- Format standardized agenda and recap documents for each meeting type, and make the templates easily accessible. In your calendar system, require one person to be selected as facilitator and one as "Recap-tain" for each meeting. Also automatically set alerts for them to send out meeting agendas and recap notes.
- Create accountability structures to follow up on action items, problems, and opportunities discussed in meetings. One way to do this is to begin each meeting with a review of the action items from the prior meeting's recap.
- Regularly seek feedback from your team on how they feel about meetings and your performance in them. Don't ask if you are "good" or "bad." Instead, inquire about the emotional impact you have. Offer them simple words such as *encouraged, productive, long, confusing, frustrating,* etc.

CHAPTER 5

Empower the Team and Hold Them Accountable

"I just play the role I can given the person and what I think they need at the moment. It could be a rookie. It could be a veteran."[1]

—Tom Brady

EMPOWERMENT TAKES MANY FORMS

Here's a scenario: you're a star quarterback in the NFL. You've lived under immense pressure since your sophomore year of high school. College coaches from the top football programs around the country pursued you. With an eye always on your ultimate goal of playing in the NFL, you selected a well-respected college program where you played in a pro-style offense. You led your team for four years, played well in bowl games, won awards, and garnered constant media attention. When it came time for the NFL draft, prognosticators and scouts fawned over your skill and poise. There was no situation too high-pressured, no scheme too complex, no window too tight for you to pinpoint a laser-like pass. You were about as highly regarded as they come, and the expectations for your professional career were sky high.

After several years in the league, you haven't just met expectations—you've exceeded them. You worked incredibly hard: you're always the first one in the practice facility, and the last one to leave the video room. You're a superlative leader in the locker room and on the field, corralling a ragtag bunch to sustained success. In every way, you've delivered.

This offseason, you finished your rookie contract, which due to NFL rules doesn't pay much. It's time for your first "real" contract, when you're finally eligible to get paid like the big boys. You've certainly earned it. Statistically, you're one of the best quarterbacks in the NFL. Schematically, you demonstrated mastery of the offense and excellent decision-making. Physically, you put on muscle and gained speed, which allowed an exciting expansion of the playbook. Your win-loss record speaks for itself. You performed well in the playoffs, and learned a great deal from your experience that will serve you well in the future.

You've more than paid your dues, and it's time to get paid. Your agent sets up a meeting in his office. You know you want to stay with the same team, but it's time to figure out exactly the terms you're looking for and determine your negotiation strategy.

"Wow, great season, buddy. You absolutely killed it out there. With your performance and upside, I think we can really get some money out of these guys," your agent crows.

"Well, I'm not trying to be selfish," you explain. "Between my salary and endorsements, I already have more money than I'll ever probably need. It's really more about what the money represents. It's a sign of respect to pay a top quarterback a top salary. The franchise sends a message that they're invested in you, that you're the team leader they're going to build around you. I want the team to send that signal."

"Of course they should!" says your agent as he slaps his desk. "You've been terrific. Plus you're still so young. They'll want to keep you happy now so you'll want to re-sign with them again later," he concludes.

"The truth is, in the back of my mind, I'm worried," you admit. "Football's violent. Quarterbacks have a target on their backs. Nothing makes a defensive lineman happier than absolutely crushing a guy into the turf. Plus these NFL contracts aren't fully guaranteed, and you never know what can happen. Joe Theismann broke his leg and never played another game. Troy Aikman and Steve Young had to stop playing because of head injuries. Sure I'm healthy now, but I'm not blind to the risk. And you know I'm getting married soon. I have to make sure my family is going to be OK if anything happens to me, or if this is my last contract," you say quietly.

Your agent has become somber.

"Don't worry," he says as he shakes his head. "We're going to get it all taken care of. You and your family will be protected," he assures.

You explore all the options with your agent and decide on a plan of action. He sets up a meeting with the team's general manager for the following week. But the next day, you hear news that changes your whole perspective: Tom Brady just signed a new contract with his team, and it's for a shockingly small number. You call your agent right away.

"What's up with this Brady contract?" you ask, confused. "Why would he do that? He's Tom Brady, for crying out loud. I know he's like a hundred years old, but he's still one of the best quarterbacks in the league. Plus, the man's a living legend."

"I know, it's crazy. And remember, this isn't the first time Brady's given his team a steep discount," your agent reminds you.

You're absolutely stunned, and thoughts about Brady's new deal swirl around your head constantly in the lead-up to your own negotiations. It seems like every time you turn around, Brady restructures his contract. He repeatedly gave up millions of dollars in salary to give the New England Patriots a manageable deal, and he was unbelievably flexible in reworking his contracts to save the Patriots salary cap space. When he signed with the Tampa Bay Buccaneers,[2] it was the largest annual salary he he had ever received, but it still didn't rank him in the top ten for quarterback salaries,[3] and left the Bucs plenty of room to build around him.

You understand reworking your contract to help the team with cap space. It gets you better teammates and doesn't really cost you money. You even understand taking a one-time pay cut to secure a phenomenal free agent that could put your team over the top. But the amount Brady gives up and the number of times he's reworked his deal is unbelievable. You look it up. In 2018, Brady was only the eighteenth-highest paid quarterback (not even overall player) in the NFL.[4] In a league of 32 teams, that would put Brady as a middling quarterback, which he certainly was not—he led his team to another Super Bowl victory that year. So what Brady does, over and over again, just doesn't make sense. You keep asking yourself, *Why? I know he's already rich. But he's basically giving money away. It seems . . . stupid. And Tom Brady is not a stupid guy.*

All week you obsess over it. Tossing and turning the night before your meeting with the general manager, you have an epiphany. The next morning, you huddle with your agent before the meeting.

"I've been thinking about it all week, and I get it now. About Brady. It all makes sense," you smile.

"OK . . ." says your agent, confused. "Care to share?"

"It's brilliant, actually," you enthuse. "The salary cap is hugely complicated. Brady giving them a break on his salary is him doing the team a solid, obviously," you state.

"Right," confirms your agent, "and it helps them build a better team around him. Although that doesn't explain why Brady's done this so many times."

"Think about the results," you tell him, "because there's actually method to the madness. In 2018, when Brady was paid like some average quarterback, the Patriots won the Super Bowl.[5] Money doesn't matter to him—it's about leading the team to victory."

"What do you mean, exactly?" your agent asks.

"Look, this is a guy who reportedly pays cash to players on the practice squad when they intercept him!"[6] you declare. "He's keeping himself publicly accountable. It sends a signal to everyone else that they better hold themselves accountable, too.

"And he's always trying to improve himself. He's a six-time champion, but he's still angry if he messes up in practice. He's showing his teammates that they need to be working just as hard on getting better," you say.

"Plus he was living everything Belichick and the Patriots are supposed to stand for. You know, 'The Patriot Way,' the team-first attitude they're famous for. By getting paid less and tinkering with his deals all the time, he's putting the team above himself. It's a sign to everyone in that locker room that they need to put the team first, too. He's demonstrating his own dedication to the team. Not even first-ballot Hall of Famer Tom Brady is bigger than the team," you emphasize.

"So, it's about accountability," your agent says.

"Right, and about empowerment and rewarding great play. Remember when he was named MVP of the 2015 Super Bowl against the Seattle Seahawks? The MVP award was a truck. Instead of keeping it, he gave it to Malcolm Butler, the no-name Pats defender who made that great interception with 20 seconds left to save the game,"[7] you recall. "Rewarding Butler is motivation for teammates to make more great plays," you conclude.

"OK," your agent says, "so what does that mean for today?"

You smile as you share your new negotiation strategy with your agent. You're going to follow Brady's example for your new contract. You'll still get paid plenty of money, and your family will be safe. But you're going to make sure your contract leaves the team in the best possible position to sign as many quality players as possible. You want to demonstrate your own dedication to the team and your teammates. The respect of your teammates comes from the leadership you display, not the zeros in your game check. Indeed, when the team gathers for the start of training camp, there's a noticeable difference in the locker room. You're now surrounded by an extremely talented group of players, and they seem especially eager to get going. Their desire and dedication is immediately visible on the field. You know you've made the right choice.

LEADERSHIP LESSONS FROM THE FIELD:

- The best leaders prove their dedication to the team in their words and actions. They are focused solely on the ultimate goal, which is reflected in how they live their lives and conduct themselves at work.
- Great leaders are great followers, too. They recognize that no one person is bigger than the team, and are willing to sacrifice personal rewards to achieve the team's goals.
- Leaders are not threatened by working with people smarter and differently talented than they are. Instead, leaders embrace and trust those people to use their unique skill sets to push the team forward.

EMPOWERMENT GENERATES SUCCESS

Brady knows that just telling people to do something won't make that thing happen. Leaders need to understand both *empowerment* and *accountability*. Only when they've mastered these concepts can they diagnose and resolve deficiencies up front, improving the likelihood of success in the future. The good news is that employee engagement in the US is rising. The bad news is that it's still at an abysmal 34 percent.[8]

Unfortunately, leaders often disempower their employees. Some leaders diminish others to promote their own self-interest, or prevent them from achieving their full potential for fear of being outshined. Poor leaders fail to recognize the contributions others make to the success of the team, making members feel unappreciated and ineffective. Studies show that employees who are disempowered are unhappier at work, and disempowered teams are less likely to achieve their goals.[9]

Great leaders like Brady, meanwhile, empower their team to the benefit of the whole group. They give their team members the skills and knowledge they need to succeed, and support them along the way. They use empowerment as a tool to build up others and help them achieve their full potential, making sure they're deeply engaged with the company and its mission. The impact of empowerment on the bottom line is dramatic: companies with more engaged workers achieve 21 percent higher profitability.[10]

Over the course of his career, Brady has shattered every assumption people made about him, and he's happy to help others do the same. He is secure enough in his own skills to let them shine. Most people rise only to their perceived limits, but Brady wants his teammates to go beyond what they thought was possible for themselves. For example, in his impactful film sessions (see Chapter 4), he points out mistakes, but more importantly gives his teammates the tools and rewards they need to perform better next time. For Brady, it's all quite logical: "In my life, winning has been a priority . . . It's a salary cap. You can only spend so much, and the more that one guy gets is less for others. And from a competitive advantage standpoint, I like to get a lot of good players around me,"[11] he says.

Leaders who empower their teams are also willing to give up control of a project to the person best suited to lead it. Brady will happily defer to the running game if that's the best strategy for the team. He's even been known to throw a block—unheard of for a quarterback, and particularly for an old and slow one—to help a play succeed. Whereas poor leaders feel the need to shine so brightly that there's no room for anyone else to get even a flicker, great leaders do everything they can to accomplish the best idea, and then bask in the glow of the people they support.

Brady also uses accountability as a tool to help his team. He sets the high standard to which he holds himself and his teammates. He doesn't expect from his teammates anything he doesn't fulfill himself. Brady's film sessions hold his offensive teammates accountable, although without shaming them. His infectious passion pushes himself and his team beyond what they imagined.

More than anything, great leaders like Brady want to win. In fact, his deference to Belichick's leadership was part of what makes Brady a great leader. Brady knew Belichick was rough around the edges, but submitted to Belichick's methods because they work. By holding himself to such high personal standards, and by being accountable to Belichick, Brady set the example for the rest of his team.

In the media, Brady talks a lot about taking pleasure in the process. He understands that the daily grind is what leads to victory, but he also understands why it's called a "grind." It's not easy to motivate yourself or others to do the work necessary for success. That's why structures of accountability and empowerment are so important. They keep team members inspired and aligned.

An important part of empowerment is communication. Team members need to know their leader believes in them and wants to support their efforts. All too often, people in business leadership positions are poor communicators. They may have other strengths, like clarity of vision or a sharply analytical mind, but unfortunately people skills are often overlooked in hiring.

This is an area where great followers can immediately make a big impact on their team and demonstrate their leadership skills. They can make up for the leader's poor communication. Any employee can set the example by turning bad communication into good execution. Just like Brady, they see through distractions to the core message of the leader, and translate it for the team into something productive and dynamic to push the whole team forward.

There are many examples of business leaders holding themselves to high standards in both their personal and professional lives. Plenty of high-profile CEOs take $1 annual salaries (admittedly they are usually compensated handsomely in other ways).[12] Renowned sales expert Jack Daly publishes specific goals before each year, and then publicly assesses his performance at the end of each year regardless of his successes and failures.[13] These actions send a signal to employees—and investors—that leaders are dedicated and willing to sacrifice for the company's success.

ACTION FROM THE BUSINESS STADIUM: ACCOUNTABILITY BEGETS EXECUTION

Without clear accountability and strong empowerment, disaster can strike a company. One government contractor with a project-driven business model discovered this the hard way.

The culture at the company had always been relaxed, and the new CEO, Peter, wanted to maintain that tradition. At the same time, he wanted to solve a problem he had noticed while working his way up through the company. Throughout his career, he often found himself placed on projects he didn't enjoy. They drained his enthusiasm, and the more time those projects took, the lower the quality of work he produced on all his concurrent projects. Just as Brady wants a happy locker room, Peter wanted a company of employees who were enthused about their jobs. Peter recognized the inefficiency in the system, and wanted to make a change. When a company-wide employee survey confirmed his feelings, Peter gathered his executive team to explain his plan.

"I've been looking at our employee satisfaction numbers, and I believe we can do better. I'm not so far removed from the same positions as many of the people we surveyed. When I was a young employee, and later as a mid-level manager, I often found myself working on projects I disliked. Sometimes it was a subject matter I wasn't thrilled about, other times it was a client I didn't care for, and sometimes it was the executive in charge who I didn't see eye-to-eye with. Those projects were real culture killers. I saw colleagues engaged in projects I yearned to dig into, working under managers I would run through a wall for. It always felt unfair that I was assigned to something I didn't specialize in, or something run by a manager I didn't jive with," Peter shared.

"There are always elements in any job that people dislike, aren't there?" asked Nathan, one of the executives.

"Sure," responded Peter, "but I think we should reduce it as much as possible. Employees in that situation are less efficient and more unhappy. Plus project managers forget how much other work individual team members already have, so people get overloaded with everything assigned to them. That hurts each project and their teams."

"So what do you propose as a solution?" asked Olivia, the vice president.

"I'm proposing that we move to a 75 percent volunteer system for projects. Employees will get to choose three-quarters of the projects they work on. They'll get to choose subject matters they're passionate about, work with clients they enjoy, and make better decisions about their workload," said Peter.

"Now, I know what you're going to say," he predicted. "What happens when no one wants to work on a particular project? But that's why the system is only 75 percent voluntary. So 25 percent of an employee's time will still be work assigned to them based on what we need," he explained, pleased with his plan.

The executives had some reservations, but not wanting to dismiss his first idea as CEO, they agreed to give Peter's proposal a try. When the change was announced, the employees were thrilled. It was as if football players were told they could skip weightlifting sessions when they wanted. Employees would now get to spend the bulk of their time on the work they cared about the most and were most qualified to do. They had more ability to say no when they felt overwhelmed. It felt liberating, and many felt it was a sign the company really believed in them and in their ability to do their jobs well without being micromanaged.

In the months after the change in assignment structure, things went well for the company. The attitude around the office was more cheerful, and people seemed enthusiastic about arriving to work every day. Many projects became more efficient almost overnight. Those clients were thrilled with how engaged the team seemed, and some clients started to contract more projects with them. Peter's tenure as CEO was off to a strong start.

Slowly, however, the luster of the new volunteer initiative started to fade. Employees' initial enthusiasm about choosing their own projects began to ebb as they grew bored working with the same people on the same types of projects. Some project managers found their motivational tools lost effectiveness as they used them repeatedly on the same people. Further, certain projects and certain managers were chronically underrepresented in the volunteer selection and relied almost exclusively on assignment. The unpopular projects felt more burdensome than ever for employees assigned to them, and performance on those projects suffered.

Olivia and Nathan were growing concerned. They could feel growing discontent among employees, saw a retreat from the efficiency the company had initially gained, and tracked reduced sales numbers from executives. Employees were no longer taking ownership of projects, even the ones they chose, and as a result, several projects fell behind schedule. Project managers previously were able to produce cohesive, consistent results for clients. But with employees only half engaged in the projects, the managers had a difficult time getting everyone aligned and producing their best work.

The volunteer scheme was starting to impact the bottom line. With missed deadlines and spotty customer service, the company was at risk of losing clients. Olivia and Nathan also noticed a slight uptick in turnover. Their experience told them things were heading in a bad direction. It was a situation Brady likely could not have tolerated, whether a team leader or team member. Olivia and Nathan decided to meet with Peter to express their concerns.

"Peter," Olivia began, "Nathan and I have been tracking carefully the implications of the volunteer structure. We're becoming concerned that it's negatively affecting the company."

"I'm surprised to hear this," Peter responded. "Everyone seemed so thrilled about it. Tell me what you mean."

"Well," said Nathan, "we're concerned that allowing people to choose the majority of their projects has created an atmosphere that is *too* relaxed. Things are starting to fall through the cracks. It's like death by a thousand cuts."

"OK, but isn't a relaxed culture a good thing?" asked Peter.

"In theory, yes," replied Nathan. "And I know we've always had a more laid-back culture. It's something employees like, and it's helped attract good talent. But it seems allowing employees to volunteer for their projects has made the work seem, well . . . voluntary. We initially saw an increase in employee satisfaction, and we made some improvements in efficiency. There was a nice jump in sales as a result. But lately, we've lost all the gains we made."

"Guys, I just finished looking at the numbers for last quarter. Things are going great!" Peter insisted.

"I know last quarter's numbers look that way," replied Olivia calmly. "But our projections for this quarter are down considerably. It's almost back to how it was before the volunteer program. And our long-term projections are worse than that."

Peter was stunned.

"Peter, I'm afraid we might need to take a step back from the volunteer system," admitted Olivia.

"But it was a good plan," Peter said, shaking his head. "And it worked right away. Don't you think this could be just a blip on the radar? A growing pain? How can you be so sure it's the volunteer initiative causing the problem?"

"We don't think it's a temporary problem," said Nathan. "We've discussed the changes in detail with our managers, and with a number of ground-level employees. The response is universally the same—the volunteer initiative hurt us. There hasn't been a change anywhere else that could account for our decreased numbers. There weren't other policy changes. No client upheaval or industry shift. It all keeps coming back to the volunteer initiative. It wasn't what anyone intended, but it's the reality."

"I hear you, I do," said Peter. "But I just can't believe it's all on the volunteer program. I'm not ready to abandon ship yet. Is there something you think we can do to fix it?"

"I guess it's possible," speculated Olivia. "I think the problem is we changed up the whole structure without putting any safeguards in place. There's no tracking system, so managers don't really have any way of holding their teams accountable. They barely even feel like teams anymore. Which means there's no peer monitoring, and less opportunity for skill reinforcement from managers. They're just collections of individuals working on loosely related tasks."

"So what if we created a progress tracking system for each project, with a breakdown of each individual's tasks?" suggested Nathan. "I know we've avoided it in the past because of our relaxed culture and fear of micromanaging, but it might be time to implement it. It would be a visual reminder to employees of what they need to do, and would give the manager better understanding of project status. And as soon as managers see something wrong, they can make sure team members have everything they need to succeed."

"I think we can make that work," stated Olivia.

Over the next several weeks, the executive team designed and implemented an accountability and empowerment program. The tracking system was simple, but worked well. It held employees to deadlines without making them feel nit-picked and still left them the freedom to schedule their time as they saw fit. The executives also planned a series of professional development courses so employees could expand their skills, rather than just stick with what they knew, and choose a wider variety of projects. The managers no one wanted to work for received leadership training to teach improved methods of engaging with employees. Just as Brady does, the executives helped employees learn to take pleasure in the process.

Slowly, performance improved. There was still a backlog to untangle and relationships to rebuild, but the company was able to stabilize employee turnover and reestablish culture, regain financial footing, and rehabilitate its reputation with clients. Eventually, the accountability and empowerment program helped Peter lead the company to achieve success even beyond what prior CEOs had managed.

MORE ACTION FROM THE BUSINESS STADIUM: ACCOUNTABILITY STARTS AT THE TOP

Even in companies with strong processes for accountability, there must be universal buy-in for the system to succeed. The experience of a digital marketing company demonstrates this necessity. A small group of investors—Caleb, Jimmy, and Sean—owned the company and decided to hire Chloe as CEO to run the business day-to-day. They trusted Chloe, but they still wanted to play a role in determining strategy and making decisions.

While the company had been well run under the old trio, Chloe believed there was room to improve the company's approach to accountability. She believed better accountability would improve efficiency, which would in turn develop trust among employees. Chloe proposed a new computer software system for the owners, executives, and senior managers. The computer program was intuitive and thorough. It allowed every team member to track their projects in detail, as well as get updates on the status of any other project.

On its launch, the program was a huge success. The executive team and senior managers loved it. They were fully aware of all the latest developments on their projects. Plus, they no longer had to wait on updates about other projects in order to continue related work in their own projects. Communication and cohesiveness among the divisions improved. Managers no longer had to pester their team members to ensure they were staying on track because they had a real-time view of each person's status. No one had to wonder what the next step was, and meetings became more useful and efficient. Deadlines were crystal clear, and the system helped the company spot potential problems far in advance, with plenty of time to solve them. Employees were more productive, and customers were thrilled with the performance.

Caleb, Jimmy, and Sean were thrilled with Chloe. She had embraced her role as CEO and was already finding success. The computer program was a boon for accountability at every level of the company. They had full faith that Chloe would put the company in the best position to succeed and could lead the company through any challenge. Chloe felt their support and began to tackle a number of other initiatives.

At first, Caleb, Jimmy, and Sean were diligent about using the computer system to track progress on their own responsibilities. Every time they used the system, they were reminded of how smoothly things were running. It made their jobs easier, gave them peace of mind, and allowed them more time to count all the money the company was making.

In fact, the system made their jobs so easy that they began to forget to update the computer system regularly. It was no big deal at first. Chloe would occasionally have to remind them to complete some routine tasks. If Chloe knew something was done and noticed they hadn't entered it into the system, she would enter it for them. Still, they would usually get things done on time, and their lack of diligence in updating the system was just a minor inconvenience for the executive team. Even Brady sometimes has to correct teammates on how they line up pre-snap or remind someone to motion behind the line of scrimmage.

Unfortunately, the owners' negligence of the computer system progressively worsened. Despite Chloe's efforts to encourage regular updates in the system, the executive team started to notice that Caleb, Jimmy, and Sean were routinely neglecting the system. Their tracking was weeks behind, and the company was starting to miss internal deadlines. The owners' apathy towards the accountability system was starting to create serious problems for Chloe and the executive team. It put Chloe in the uncomfortable position of serving as a taskmaster to her bosses. It also undermined Chloe's ability to enforce regular updates from her team, since everyone could see that her bosses weren't making their updates. Even as prepared as Brady is, it would be more difficult for him to take his teammates to task if the head coach started slacking in his duties. As the bottleneck worsened, Chloe could see her team's enthusiasm for the system fading. Things were beginning to backslide, and Chloe knew she had to stop the bleeding. She called a meeting with Caleb, Jimmy, and Sean.

"Gentlemen, we've talked about this a number of times before, but the problem has now reached a critical mass: it is absolutely essential that you start entering your progress into the computer tracking system. You need to do it every single day without fail. It's affecting our bottom line," she scolded.

"Yes, of course, we've talked about this plenty," responded Caleb, slightly annoyed. "We're not perfect in our use, but tracking our progress was never a problem before we had the system. We're still getting things done on time, mostly. This can't be that big of a deal, and frankly, it's getting a little tiring to hear about it," he sighed.

"You say it's impacting the bottom line," stated Jimmy. "How so? Seems hard to believe such a little thing could have that kind of effect."

"But that's exactly it, guys," said Chloe. "Everyone else has been using the system diligently. It's really revolutionized the way divisions are able to work together. Teams are meeting deadlines consistently, sometimes even *early*. My executives and I can spend our meetings tackling important issues, instead of just getting each other caught up on where each project stands. Frontline employees know exactly what to say to customers who request updates. The system has smoothed our operations dramatically. Employees and customers are happy.

"Here's what's creating the problems," she continued. "When you three don't input your progress, the executives and senior managers don't know whether you've done your work and whether they can move on to the next step in the project. They don't want to bother you, so they waste time avoiding it, and finally, when it's almost too late, they start demanding attention. Then they have to scramble to catch up," Chloe explains.

"OK, but they are catching up, right? I still don't see how it's impacting our bottom line," challenged Sean.

"They're usually able to, but it's been close—too close— several times. You're creating a bottleneck, and one day soon it's going to break," Chloe asserted.

"And there's more," she stated. "The executives, senior managers, and I have been having these really productive meetings. We don't have to spend time anymore updating each other on operations. Everyone already knows all that stuff. Instead, we have time to talk about solving problems and setting long-term agendas."

"Well that's great," offered Sean.

"Right, it is great," Chloe continued. "The executive team is drama-free, and relationships with senior managers are better than ever. And so they assume that our meetings together, just the four of us, are equally productive. They think I'll be able to bring them important information based on our discussions. But I can't give them anything because we seem to spend all our meeting time with me badgering you about updating the computer system and then getting you up to speed on projects. The executives are frustrated that I don't have more direction for them, a clearer vision of what's to come. Their expectations are higher now. That should be a good thing, but since we aren't delivering on those expectations, morale is suffering, and they're losing faith in me," Chloe admitted.

"Here's what's going to happen—and I know, because it's already started. My executives are going to get tired of using a tracking system that doesn't work because the leaders don't use it. They're going to get complacent about it, just like you have, and they're going to get lazy about updating it. And that's going to create a situation far worse than it was before we had the system, because inevitably wires are going to get crossed about which department's using it and which isn't. At least before, no one was using the system, so everyone knew they had to dig for updates. All the cohesion and efficiency we've built is going to fall apart, and we'll be worse off than when we started," Chloe warned.

"Can't you prevent that from happening by just continuing to enforce the system?" asked Caleb.

"I can try," Chloe said. "But it's a lot harder to hold them accountable to the system when leaders at the top aren't doing it. They won't miss the irony that you're not being held accountable on a program designed to improve *accountability*."

Caleb, Jimmy, and Sean were silent. They had no idea the impact their nonchalance had on the company. Instead of setting the example and maintaining the highest standards like Brady would, they put themselves above the team. They felt bad their employees held up their end of the bargain while the three of them failed. And Chloe was in a bind they created. The three owners discussed the problem and agreed to demonstrate accountability by regularly updating the tracking system.

Slowly, things started to turn around. Caleb, Jimmy, and Sean rededicated themselves to the system and reserved time on their daily calendars to submit updates. As the owners caught up on their tracking and the system became useful again, members of Chloe's team revived their own commitment to the program. Eventually, the system became more successful than ever as everyone in the company, from top to bottom, participated fully.

GAME REVIEW:

- When leaders empower their team members, they must simultaneously hold them accountable. Poor accountability in one area can infect other business operations and cause major problems.

(Continued on next page)

- Leaders set the standard for the rest of the team. Initiatives without buy-in from leadership are destined to fail. Even the most relaxed cultures need structures that keep everyone, from top management to entry-level employees, fully accountable for their responsibilities.

EXECUTING THE PLAY

Exercises for the Preseason:

- Consider your reaction if your boss gave you the last instructions you gave a member of your team. Would you feel you had the authority to align resources and complete the task? If something went wrong, would you believe your boss would support you in solving the problem without micromanaging or taking over? How can you change your behavior so your employees are better empowered to do their jobs?
- Do you have an accountability system in your company? If not, why not? Have there been any recent miscommunications or mistakes that could have been avoided if there were a system? Design what your ideal system might look like. It doesn't have to be complicated or expensive, but it needs to be easy to access and intuitive to use. How could you implement this program?

Best Practices for the Game:

- Empower your people by ensuring they have the tools they need to take action. Make sure they know they have your support without making them feel you're babysitting them.
- Hold yourself to the same high standards to which you hold team members. It's meaningful when leaders play by the same rules and inspires team members to do the same.

CHAPTER 6

Always Prepare for Crisis

"We played one of the best teams that I've ever played against. I think that's really where Patriots football and team football really kind of started for us in New England. It took a team effort to win that game."[1]

—Tom Brady, on his first Super Bowl victory

ORGANIZATIONAL DISARRAY BRINGS ON-FIELD FAILURE

Football is arguably the ultimate team sport. An NFL roster has 53 men, with several more on the practice squad. There are innumerable assistant coaches, strength and conditioning coaches, nutrition experts, equipment managers, and many others required to make a team function, not to mention the front office administration, facilities coordinators, scouts, and ownership. A professional football team is a huge operation. Even after the game begins, the team can only achieve success if 11 men on the field work in almost perfect coordination. With so much going on, it's not hard to see how easily things can go wrong. Sadly for local fans, some NFL franchises seem particularly adept at finding opportunities for failure.

The 2008 AFC Eastern Division demonstrated a most striking contrast of crisis leadership. Comparing the New York Jets to their division rival Patriots bears strong lessons. The Jets couldn't get a highly talented group of players to perform well. The Patriots, meanwhile, saw less talented players perform well beyond expectations. The difference in these organizations' leadership and crisis management skills was stark.

The 2008 New York Jets were an example of the kind of disastrous crisis management that plagues poor teams. Just two seasons prior, in 2006, things were looking up for Gang Green. They went 10–6 under first-year head coach Eric Mangini,[2] whom fans called the "Mangenius."[3] Quarterback Chad Pennington was a revelation and earned the NFL Comeback Player of the Year Award.[4] The Jets made the playoffs,[5] and the team was looking forward to carrying that momentum into the following season. Unfortunately for the Jets, 2007 did not turn out the way they planned. They regressed to a terrible 4–12 record,[6] and never came close to their 2006 level.

Despite a poor 2007, Jets fans and the organization still felt positive going into the 2008 season. In addition to Pennington, the Jets had several young Pro Bowl-caliber players who were playing great.[7] In the offseason, the team spent a great deal of money to acquire a number of players who would make major improvements to the offensive line.[8] Observers could chalk up Mangini's 2007 performance to a classic "sophomore slump" that he would overcome in his third year as coach. With a talented roster, a more experienced coach, a new stadium under construction, and a new team headquarters just about to open,[9] there were real reasons for optimism.

Then came a stunning, monster move that made fans wildly excited: the Jets acquired superstar quarterback Brett Favre in a trade with the Green Bay Packers. The Jets swiftly cut Chad Pennington to make room for Favre, a living legend. When he got to the Jets, Favre had a Super Bowl ring, was a nine-time Pro Bowler, and had three regular season MVP Awards.[10] Just the year prior, Favre led his Packers to the NFC Championship Game.[11] Imagine the damage Favre could do behind the Jets' now-formidable offensive line!

Amid eager anticipation and fanfare, the 2008 season began well for the Jets. Favre was proving to be worth it: in Week

4, he threw a career-high six touchdown passes.[12] After Week 12, the team was 8–3.[13] Players thought they had something special, and right tackle Damien Woody recalled, "We honestly felt like we had a team that could go to the Super Bowl."[14] Jets fans were delirious with joy.

Just when the going got good, seemingly out of nowhere, the season imploded. The Jets suddenly couldn't do anything right. Favre started throwing interceptions left and right, and the team lost three of its next four games. It was an utter collapse. However, going into the last game of the regular season, the Jets still had a chance to make the playoffs. All they had to do was win a home game against the Miami Dolphins, now quarterbacked by Jets castoff Chad Pennington. In a torturous moment for Jets management and fans, they lost the game—and the playoff spot—to Pennington and the Dolphins.[15, 16] By missing the playoffs, all the excitement generated in the off-season was for naught. After the season, Favre told the Jets he would retire,[17] and the team fired Eric Mangini. What could have been a storybook season instead became an infamous failure.

How had such a promising Jets season gone so awry? As it turned out, there had been many warning signs. Green Bay traded away Favre not because he was playing poorly, but because the organization was tired of his seasons-long public indecision over retirement. Favre's attitude suggested insufficient dedication to football and handcuffed the Packers from making long-term decisions. Additionally, Mangini wanted no part of Favre, believing Favre's star status would damage the team-first mentality Mangini was trying to build.[18] Despite conventional wisdom that owners without football backgrounds shouldn't overrule football decision-makers, Jets ownership traded for Favre anyway.[19] Then they had to cut Pennington to make room on the roster, leaving the team without an experienced backup quarterback despite their starter's advanced age. Further, Mangini essentially threw out his entire playbook to center the system around Favre,[20] who begged for the offense to be simplified.[21] Mangini, who came up the NFL ranks under no-nonsense Bill Belichick, also lightened the team practice load because Favre didn't want to spend so much time on the field.[22] Completely changing one's coaching style to accommodate a single player was a risky move. The Jets had a golden opportunity for success in 2008, but bungled the project badly by setting themselves up for failure before the season began. Their decisions left them totally unprepared for any unexpected challenges.

Like the Jets, the Patriots' 2008 season also started with high expectations. The 2007 Patriots were one of the best teams in the history of the NFL. They went 16–0 in a dominating regular season, and Brady threw a record 50 touchdowns on his way to becoming the runaway MVP. The Pats performed well in the playoffs and were heavily favored to beat the New York Giants in Super Bowl XLII. In one of the biggest upsets in Super Bowl history, the Giants shocked the Patriots to win, 17-14. So when the 2008 season began, the Patriots, who returned with basically the same team intact, were out for revenge.

The Patriots' 2008 season opened with a game at home against the Kansas City Chiefs. Brady, who for several *seasons* had appeared each week on the team injury report, and who had missed all the preseason games with a foot injury, was finally healthy enough not to merit a slot on that week's injury report.[23] Just five minutes into the first quarter, Brady had already completed six of ten passes and was well on his way to another stellar performance.[24]

And then, silence. On a deep pass to wide receiver Randy Moss, Brady took a hit to the legs from Kansas City safety Bernard Pollard. Brady crumbled to the ground, and the Gillette Stadium crowd froze motionless, not even caring that Moss had fumbled the ball. The training staff rushed to Brady's aid. With their help, Brady managed to hobble off the field, but everyone suspected the worst. Later that week, those fears were confirmed: Brady had torn both the ACL and MCL in his left knee, and would miss the remainder of the season.[25]

From that point, it would have been easy for the 2008 Patriots to implode just like the Jets had. The reigning NFL MVP and the Patriots' undisputed leader was gone. His replacement, Matt Cassel, wasn't exactly a hot quarterback commodity. He hadn't started a football game at quarterback since high school; he was a backup for his entire career at the University of Southern California and had barely seen the field in his time in the NFL.[26] But throwing in the towel is not how the Patriots go about their business.

It seemed the Patriots' team mantra of "Do Your Job" had never been on such public display. Ownership trusted head coach Bill Belichick to keep the ship upright, and Belichick maintained his same steady demeanor, consistent messaging, and relentless work ethic.[27] The organization was always ready for a crisis, and even losing Brady would not catch them unprepared.

The Patriots designed their organization with the understanding that working hard was important, but working smart was even more so. They had a solid play scheme and a well-established routine that made dealing with crises simple. The Patriots had a complete team with largely interchangeable pieces. With their excellent communication and practice habits, everyone understood and met expectations. They were well practiced in accommodating unexpected changes, and this situation proved to be no different.

Belichick designed the team to be consistent and resilient. Even with Brady injured, Belichick barely had to change the offense at all to accommodate Cassel.[28] While Cassel was a no-name player, the Patriots' careful evaluation of his skills and their diligent, consistent preparation meant he was immediately ready to lead the team in Brady's sudden absence.

Committed to the Patriots' approach and to his team, Brady no doubt contributed effectively even from off the field. After his surgery, Brady was at the Patriots' practice facility, upbeat and encouraging his teammates in the locker room.[29] Although Belichick asked him to stay off the sidelines during games so as not to create a media distraction, Brady was still a regular presence at the practice facility.[30] His teammates saw Brady working hard on his rehab, which kept them motivated, and he helped them maintain perspective on how lucky they were to be playing football. Brady also seemed to continue to support Cassel and the offense with his knowledge, experience, and insights.

With good organizational structure from top to bottom, the 2008 Patriots ended the season with an 11–5 record. Although they missed the playoffs, they were only the second team in the entire history of the NFL to miss the playoffs after winning 11 games.[31] Teams in the same division play nearly identical schedules, and the 2008 Patriots, led by a no-name quarterback, outperformed the superstar-laden 2008 Jets. Ultimately, the difference came down to preparatory crisis management.

Brady, Belichick, and the Patriots demonstrated that organization by design can adapt to any situation and manage any challenge. By carefully crafting a complete team and ensuring thorough preparation at every level, the Patriots could handle any crisis that came their way. Despite missing their most important player on the field, their preparation allowed them to raise their level of play individually and collectively to succeed in even the most difficult scenario. Time and again, "The Patriot Way" has proven to be a path to sustained success.

Beyond just the 2008 season, Brady's proactive commitment to preparation allows for his amazing adaptability in the face of crisis. The time he puts into studying and decision-making off the field makes him ready for anything on the field. When someone on Brady's offensive line suffers an injury midweek, Brady doesn't have to panic. He can take the time to adjust assignments and play call plans because he has all his other responsibilities taken care of. If an opponent pulls off a surprise trade for a deadly defensive weapon, Brady knows exactly when he'll be able to study film and communicate what he learned to his offensive line.

The Patriots' structured approach also helped them avoid locker room crises. It allowed them not only to keep the peace, but also to incorporate even the most challenging player personalities. For example, Randy Moss, although a Hall-of-Fame-caliber wide receiver, was dogged by endless locker room drama with all of his prior teams. Yet in New England he flourished, with no hint of scandal. Boisterous players like Rob Gronkowski, who had perhaps the biggest, wildest personality in the NFL, played a critical role in several Patriots Super Bowls.

The Patriots' ability to create stars out of nobodies was also a cause and effect of avoiding locker room strife. The team avoided losses—and the locker room problems they bring—by embracing a culture of careful evaluation and thorough preparation. As a result, the whole roster was complementary, and every player was ready to perform at any given time. The team did not need to panic when a critical player suffered an injury. Further, the meritocracy built by the preparation smoothed transitions between players by reducing the likelihood of injured egos. After 20 years of witnessing its effectiveness, it's likely Brady will work with coaches and teammates to inspire a similar attitude in Tampa.

Brady's preparation is highly purposeful. He uses it not only to ready for the next opponent, but also to ensure the team's ability to masterfully manage whatever problems arise during the week or during the game. As a result of Brady's methods, his whole organization is aligned behind the goal of smooth process for the purpose of crisis management.

LEADERSHIP LESSONS FROM THE FIELD:

- Well-designed teams do not need to panic in a crisis. They use their extensive preparation to handle the problem in stride, and continue to learn from their experiences.
- Following a strict routine to complete your regularly required tasks will better enable you to face whatever challenges arise.

MASTER CRISIS LEADERSHIP,
EVEN WITHOUT AN NFL FRANCHISE BEHIND YOU

The crisis leadership skills Brady brings to his professional life are some of the most important a leader can bring to a company, yet most teams don't fully understand the critical value of those skills until it's too late.[32] Whether going after a client, starting an internal initiative, or expanding into a new market, every step a leader takes in business should involve awareness of and preparation for potential problems. Waiting until you're knee-deep in a project to figure out the problem-solving process is a sure path to failure.

It's naïve to be optimistic and think every project will turn out as you imagine it. The key to success is taking a pragmatic approach and focusing on what might go wrong. In fact, only 2.5 percent of companies complete their projects 100 percent successfully; the rest all fail to meet some target, budget, or deadline.[33]

Any project has a number of variables to think through *before* you begin. Even the smallest projects have to fit into the greater mission of the company. Resources are required usually from multiple departments, and the leader must keep everyone aligned while supporting production. With projects of such size and scope, the reality is that things are likely to go awry at some point. Before something goes wrong, great leaders have designed a team and process capable of tackling any obstacles encountered.

Granted, Brady has the full resources of an entire football franchise backing him up. Still, anyone can develop smart strategy, establish excellent routine, and nurture strong problem-solving skills in their workplace. Creating a systematic approach to everyday processes and problem-solving strategies enables you and your team to meet any challenge.

Good design is relatively simple at a high level. Imagine and chart out a complete vision. Break it down into manageable steps, account for the unaccountable, and rehearse with the team. There's no need to reinvent the wheel every time. Anticipating problems allows you to prepare for them. Erratic firefighting sucks up valuable time and resources. The best leaders develop and practice a consistent process they can apply to any project to move it along from start to finish, no matter the constraints.

Much like Brady, you, too, can design routine to prevent crises. The best leaders leave little to chance: they use routine to control everything they can control, so they can deal with everything else that almost surely will come along. Inadequate and inconsistent planning creates confusion and distraction, often resulting in missed milestones and frustration. On average, more than 10 percent of the money invested in a project is wasted due to poor project and crisis management skills.[34]

Although it may sound counterintuitive, routine will set you free to manage problems. You should do everything you possibly can according to a tested, trusted routine. Routines provide control. They allow you full command over everything you can control, and in an efficient manner, so that you can handle the things that come up that you cannot control.

ACTION FROM THE BUSINESS STADIUM: PROJECT MANAGEMENT THROUGH A CRISIS

Megan was the new CEO of a company distributing health-care supplies to hospitals and doctor's offices all over the United States. The company prided itself on being well run and developing leadership talent internally. Megan came up through the company and had worked in several divisions, giving her a solid grasp of the company as a whole. In her brief tenure as CEO, Megan had already improved several key metrics related to customer service and productivity, and she was now investing money to strengthen and deepen company culture.

Megan had several major initiatives she wanted to implement. One, however, was most important to her, because she felt it was most important to the company: implementing a new project management system. With a history of investing in leadership development, the company had avoided major problems in supply chain management and product distribution. Whenever an issue arose, company leaders were able to problem-solve on the fly and avert catastrophe. Still, Megan saw how close to disaster they came several times in the past.

The crisis usually started as something small, such as a typo in a product order. But as the projects got further along and the errors still weren't caught, the problems magnified. The company had no comprehensive project management system to track progress, control quality, keep the team on a deadline, and prevent errors. Megan knew that such a system would catch mistakes earlier, thereby avoiding the scramble later. For Megan, this system was a basic necessity to protect the company and its customers, and ultimately the sick patients they served.

Megan was surprised to receive some pushback when she introduced the idea at the next executive team meeting. Many of the executives knew about the close calls in the past, but believed implementing a new system was unnecessary.

"Are we going to get a bespoke computer system? How much is that going to cost?" asked one vice president.

"Tracking all these elements sounds like a bulky process that could actually slow everything down," complained another. Megan listened to and understood their concerns, but was undeterred.

"What happens," she proposed, "when our ad hoc internal problem solving fails? It will eventually happen. Even great leaders like we have in this company make mistakes sometimes. Things fall through the cracks. So far, we've been lucky. We can't rely on that forever."

The executives knew she was right and eventually agreed with her assessment. They formed a committee to explore a solution and went right to work. A few months later, they selected a project management software program they believed was cost-effective, but also allowed for enough individualization to be a good fit for the company. To make sure it was something they wanted to invest in, Megan proposed rolling out the system first to the executive team only. It would be voluntary for now, so those interested could help determine its value and work out any kinks. Then the executive team could decide whether to invest in the software company-wide.

The executives who chose to implement the new project management system were pleasantly surprised by its effectiveness. It took a while to get used to the routine of entering progress on each aspect of their projects, and it required dedicated time each day to keep the system updated. Still, overall they found the system relatively easy to use and more helpful than they expected. In fact, it was such a hit that by the end of the first month, nearly all the executives had chosen to use it.

Megan was delighted with the progress executives had made. Over the next several months, as they began planning for the company-wide rollout, Megan and the executives built up the project management system with as much data as they could. The program revealed some existing holes and weak links in their supply chain, and it reminded them of some potential customers that could be very valuable for the company. With the new system, the executives could take full control of their divisions and lead them better than ever. Things were going great, and like with Brady's teams, employees at every level were excited about the new program and embraced its importance.

Then, like Brady's knee injury, the earthquake came. It was a devastating natural disaster, right in the heart of the region from which Megan's company—and indeed, the industry—sourced many of its most important medical supplies. Thankfully the loss of life was minimal. Still, entire factories were destroyed in a matter of just a few minutes. Inventory and capability disappeared overnight. The entire medical supplies industry would soon feel the aftershocks.

Megan and her executive team sprang into action. They immediately found their new project management system prepared them well for just such an emergency event. With all the information on their supply chain entered into the new system, they had plenty of inventory on hand from which they could still supply customers. The system had recently helped them identify an unrelated shortage of a particular product, so they had developed a relationship with a manufacturer in another location that wasn't impacted by the earthquake. After the disaster, Megan was able to build on that relationship to get first dibs on other needed supplies, which were now much harder to find. Finally, the executives were able to trade existing less critical inventory for goods from competitors who were experiencing their own earthquake-related shortages.

Customers were delighted that Megan's company was able to keep them in good supply, from the moment the emergency struck and throughout the ordeal while production was rebuilt. Other hospital networks saw the amazing service received by Megan's customers and decided to switch to Megan's company, which had been so reliable under such difficult circumstances. By getting the executives to work together on a common goal, Megan and the project management system bolstered the company's bottom line and improved its standing in the industry. The project management system made the company well prepared for an emergency, and then continued to help build the company for years to come.

Tom Brady and CEO Megan both understand that robust routines keep them fully in control of their many responsibilities. Resources are regularly aligned and realigned as an ongoing part of their routine, well before a problem ever arises. When a new challenge comes, they know they can handle it because everything else is already in good working order. Their teammates, too, understand the importance of project management and its role in avoiding crises, and adhere to similar structures. They are always ready to tackle any problem and seize any opportunity.

GAME REVIEW:

- Firefighting is an inefficient method of problem solving. Leaders need to have full control over what can be controlled so they can manage whenever crises arise.
- Leaders prepare their company for every possible contingency and ensure each member of their team understands those plans.
- Great leaders find a way to transform challenges into advantages and find the opportunities in setbacks.

EXECUTING THE PLAY

Exercises for the Preseason:

- Evaluate risk thoroughly. What internal or external events could influence your team negatively? Where are you vulnerable? How can you strengthen your defenses against poor outcomes?
- Do you have a standardized project management planning system? If not, create one. Share it with your team, explain its benefits, and have them practice using it.
- If you're not sure how to develop a routine, start small. Each night before bed, write a list of everything you must accomplish the next day, in priority order. The next morning, tackle each one by one, systematically. Even this simple routine will help pave the way for more sophisticated structures.

Best Practices for the Game:

- Develop a solid routine for every day and for the responsibilities you must regularly complete. Taking control of everything in your power frees you up to tackle the unexpected.
- Stay calm in a crisis. Rely on your extensive preparation and practice to guide you out of trouble.

PART III
Firing Up the Team

CHAPTER 7

Trust Is the Twelfth Man

"I've always felt when a team trusts you to be a quarterback and they put the ball in your hands, it's a great show of trust they have in you, and I think that you need to earn it every day."[1]
—Tom Brady

FOR BRADY, TRUST IS A COMMUNICATION PRIORITY

Envision being a professional football player. You've been playing football since age five. It was your first love, a way you connected with your dad, the source of some of your closest friends. You were pretty good, actually, starting three years in high school and getting attention from some major college programs. You decided to attend a middle-tier school where you could get a great education and start all four years. It worked out great, and you had a prolific college career, even if all your games weren't against the strongest teams in the country.

You didn't get a ton of attention from NFL scouts, but still wanted to give professional football a shot. Unsurprisingly, you went undrafted, but you worked out for several teams, eventually making it onto a practice squad and, eventually, an official roster spot. You've been playing in the NFL for four seasons now, consistently making the team, even if you are almost always the last guy *not* to get cut. You're a nobody, but you're a nobody on an NFL roster, and you're having experiences you can tell your children about one day.

You've been traded twice before, and this time, you were traded to the New England Patriots. It's a safe bet you weren't the centerpiece of the deal, but at least you weren't a deal breaker for Bill Belichick, who is not just an excellent coach but also a legendary talent scout and GM. There's already a veteran star at your position, so you know you won't see the field much, but you're thrilled to be with the Patriots. You've always wanted to know how a winning culture like the one in New England would be different from the clunkers you've already experienced.

You're pumped and ready to roll. You've been preparing harder than usual, approaching the new challenge with vigor. Most of all, you don't want to embarrass yourself. Quarterback Tom Brady may be Belichick's most famous player, but Brady's on offense. As a defender, you know Belichick's specialty has always been defense. You may be an unheralded player, but you take pride in your craft. You're looking forward to working for such a brilliant defensive mind.

On the morning of your first day, you arrive at the practice facility and take a look around. You say hi to a few teammates and assistant coaches you know from college and from stints with other NFL teams. As a journeyman, you've managed to make a number of friends throughout the league. You're used to the politics of the locker room, and you know your place in a world of superstars and no names. You have no problem with that—you just want to have fun playing football.

You find your locker and get dressed for a workout in the weight room. Just as you're finishing, you hear from behind someone say your name loudly, followed by an enthusiastic,

"Hey!"

You turn around, not sure if it's directed at you, and find yourself face to face with Tom Brady, the Golden Boy himself. He's smiling, with a hand outstretched.

"Hey," he repeats, "I'm Tom Brady."[2]

You subtly look around to make sure he's talking to you and not someone else, even though he's right in front of you and making eye contact.

Why is Tom Brady talking to me? You wonder. No star player on your other teams ever bothered with anything more than a nod of the head, if that, which was just fine by you. *Maybe he's confused me for someone else,* you think. But when Brady doesn't look away, you shake his hand, befuddled.

"Nice to meet you. Glad to have you here," Brady says, and you manage to squeak out a feeble thanks before he smiles again and goes on his way.

What just happened? Why did Tom Brady, the winningest quarterback in the NFL, just come up to you on your first day and introduce himself as if you wouldn't know him? Why did he behave like he's any other player, when he so clearly is not? He's a superstar who plays on the other side of the ball, who also happens to be more than 15 years your senior. There's no reason for him even to notice you. And yet he recognized your face and knew your name, and came over to introduce himself and welcome you to the team.

Later that morning, you watch as Brady introduces himself to another new member of the team, a rookie who will play on special teams. He appears as dumbfounded as you by Brady's welcome. This is another guy Brady has no need to get to know. The kid was barely born when Brady began his career. They'll likely never share the field. Despite it all, Brady introduces himself with the same humility, respect, and authenticity he had with you.

For the rest of the day, you reflect on Brady's behavior and continue to watch him closely as you get acclimated to the team. He seems to be friendly with everyone, from coaches to players to equipment managers. No one treats him like a star who can't be approached, because he doesn't behave like one. You see a backup lineman go to Brady's locker to ask him a question about a play, and Brady stops what he's doing to focus on his concerns. You listen as Brady freely gives his time to a guy who only plays a few downs a game, even extends the conversation by pointing out a similar structure in other plays. It doesn't seem to matter to Brady who the player is; he still listens carefully and takes them seriously.

It becomes obvious to you that Brady respects his teammates. He trusts they're working hard and contributing their best effort to the team and that they're worthy of Brady's investment of time in them. By introducing himself to even the lowliest of new guys, Brady is welcoming them into the fold, demonstrating his respect for and trust in all his teammates. You're struck by how impactful that attitude is. With one introduction, you feel more welcomed on your first day with the Patriots than you did after whole seasons with other teams. Bolstered by Brady's show of confidence and trust in you and inspired by his attitude, you go on to have a career-best year with the Patriots.

LEADERSHIP LESSONS FROM THE FIELD:

- Building trust requires treating people with respect. Demonstrate that respect with your words and your actions.
- Great leaders recognize that nothing gets done without a team effort. Even seemingly unimportant teammates play a role in the team's success, and they should be treated accordingly.

THE TEAMWORK OF INFORMATION

If you pay attention to pop culture in the US, you probably know who Tom Brady is. He's one of the most famous men on the planet. He's won six Super Bowls. He's been on *People*'s Sexiest Men Alive list and named *GQ*'s Man of the Year. He wrote a *New York Times* bestseller. He's a regular attendee of the Met Ball. He's married to an actual supermodel who's both more famous worldwide and far wealthier than he is.

Of course, if you play in the NFL, you know exactly who Tom Brady is—not because of his celebrity, but because of his performance on the field. You've watched him pick apart defenses and win championships. He's been playing in the NFL so long, he may even have been your childhood hero. He's a superstar of the highest order. Brady does not need to introduce himself to anyone in any NFL locker room—and yet he does. Rookies, journeymen, and established stars all tell the same story: Brady knew exactly who they were, sight unseen, and made a point of greeting them and introducing himself. There was no hint of pretense or ego, just a genuine smile and a welcoming handshake.

How could it be that such a huge superstar has such a low-key demeanor? Brady grew up in upper middle class California and was educated at elite schools, but gets along perfectly well with teammates from inner cities and rural towns who attended the school of hard knocks. Brady is in his forties, a veteran player and family man with a luxurious lifestyle, but still connects on and off the field with teammates half his age. One of the keys to this cohesion is Brady's ability to communicate trust.

If you think about Patriots rosters over the past 20 years, it's no surprise that their leader trusted his teammates. Brady and Belichick regularly made household names of players without any history of top-tier performance.[3] Players such as Danny Woodhead, Julian Edelman, LeGarrette Blount, Dion Lewis, and many more were nobodies until they played for New England, where their careers exploded. It's hard to make such a leap in performance if you don't feel trusted by the team leader. The Pats were often able to handle "locker room problem" players[4] like Randy Moss. The Patriots even managed huge personalities like Rob Gronkowski. Belichick isn't known as a laissez-faire coach, but Belichick and Brady trusted Gronkowski to be serious when necessary, and to use his exuberance for the good of the team.

It's been said that Tom Brady treats every teammate with respect. He immediately makes every teammate feel part of the organization, a subtle but meaningful display of trust in the new player. It's a feeling Brady cultivates from the very day a new player arrives at the practice facility.

If players are treated with the same distrust or indifference they've met in the past, their behavior and play are unlikely to change. Employees whose leaders treat them with respect are 63 percent more satisfied with their jobs, 55 percent more engaged, and 110 percent more likely to stay with that organization.[5] Similarly, employees at high-trust companies experience 74 percent less stress, 106 percent more energy at work, 50 percent higher productivity, 76 percent more engagement, 29 percent more satisfaction with their lives, and 40 percent less burnout.[6] It's no surprise, then, that Moss never caused locker room strife in New England and that Woodhead demonstrated his full potential.

Brady manifests his trust in teammates in ways big and small. In press conferences, he doesn't blame teammates for losses, but instead often takes the blame himself. Sometimes during games, Brady yells at his team on the sidelines and demands better performance. Yet off the field, he's a different guy. He knows that at the next day's meeting, yelling won't help. So when he leads meetings, he speaks softly and encouragingly (see Chapter 2). Brady doesn't shy away from uncomfortable conversations or hesitate to point out mistakes, but he does so in a way that builds trust instead of criticizing harshly. He believes his teammates will learn from their mistakes and put that knowledge to good use. In offseason workouts, he apologizes profusely when a throw is even slightly off,[7] putting the blame on himself even when the ball hits the receiver's hands.

Brady also demonstrates his own trust in team leadership, which shows his teammates they should trust the leaders, too. He willingly took verbal abuse from Bill Belichick (which we'll discuss in Chapter 11). He embraces his own failures, and both learns from and uses them as motivation to improve. Brady also regularly accepts less money from his team than he could get elsewhere, proving he puts the team first, and trusts the organization to use the savings to sign other great players who will be critical to the team's success. He recognizes he cannot win alone.

In sports and in business, teamwork lives and dies on shared information. Leaders need to learn foundational communication techniques that build trust and inspire personal and professional growth. Great leaders become masters of as many communication tools as possible. They make sure everyone is on the same page. Besides, who wants to do business with or for someone they don't trust? When leaders don't trust employees, performance suffers. Whether it's demonstrated in word or deed, appearing untrustworthy is a fast track to no deal, or worse, a bad deal.

ACTION FROM THE BUSINESS STADIUM: DISTRUST BREEDS DYSFUNCTION

A digital marketing company owned by Luke and Madison was in the process of acquiring and merging with another company. As part of the process, Luke and Madison conducted a self-assessment to see how they could improve their performance and leadership. They decided that they were causing problems: they were too mired in day-to-day operations, and they weren't spending enough time on big-picture responsibilities. They needed to delegate some of their daily duties. It was a frank, honest analysis of their own performance and a wise decision.

In response, Luke and Madison created a president role and promoted an existing executive, Regan, to the position. Regan would function as the day-to-day boss and lead the newly formed management team, while Luke and Madison would have a higher-level supervisory role, functioning somewhat like a board of directors. Luke and Madison had the right intentions and made some smart moves: they recognized they were not the best people to lead the new executive team and found someone well suited to the role. They believed Regan was the right person for the job, and indeed she was.

Like leaders on a football team, the new management team had a lot to deal with. While merging the companies, a difficult task in any environment, the members of the new management team had to get to know each other and learn to work well together. They needed to develop cohesion and build trust. Regan had years of experience in executive roles, understood every aspect of the company, and had the right personality for the job. She had a plan of attack and a vision for the future that Luke and Madison agreed with and approved.

The problem was that Luke and Madison did not actually trust Regan to fulfill her duties. Trust requires action, not just words. On an intellectual level, they recognized her skill, but they had emotional difficulty trusting anyone else to lead the company they founded and grew. While they verbally said they trusted her, their actions said differently. Imagine if Patriots owner Robert Kraft didn't allow Belichick to be involved in drafting players, or if Belichick hadn't allowed Brady to make adjustments at the line of scrimmage. From the beginning, Luke and Madison unintentionally undermined Regan. Instead of empowering her to lead, they would challenge her on every small step she took, or suddenly say no to initiatives they had previously approved.

Despite the roadblocks Luke and Madison placed in front of her, Regan was doing a good job as president. She instituted open communication among the new management team and was creating cohesion. Still, Luke and Madison would constantly shift gears, pull their support, and change their minds. They would demand immediate attention on one initiative, then suddenly decide a different one deserved priority, which meant Regan had to abandon progress and reorganize the executives around a new goal. For example, Luke and Madison approved Regan's plan for occasional employee telework, but panicked at the first small misstep and rescinded the program, even though Regan warned them to expect growing pains. The inconsistency damaged Regan's credibility with her executives, and caused the team to fall behind on achieving the vision Luke and Madison desired.

Regan could see what was happening. She recognized it must have been difficult for any owner to hand over company reins to someone else. She also knew that if Luke and Madison didn't permit her to do her job, she would be unable to build the cooperation and momentum necessary for the company to achieve its major goals. Like Brady, to quarterback her team successfully, Regan needed her head coaches to let her play. Regan set up a meeting with Luke and Madison to share her concerns.

"Luke and Madison," Regan began, "we've worked together for a long time. We know each other well and understand each others' decision-making processes and motivations. In the past, we usually trusted each other to make the right business decisions. And if we ever disagreed, we handled it immediately and frankly. No backstage drama. And the company and our relationship have always come out better for it."

Luke and Madison, listening closely, agreed.

"So I'm concerned about what's happening so far in this new arrangement," Regan continued. "I'm supposed to be the president of the company. You asked me to use my industry experience, my deep understanding of this company, my rapport with employees, and our own strong relationship to make the merger seamless and productive," she said.

"That's right," said Luke, "and even though it's been off to something of a rocky start, it's not an easy thing you've been asked to do," while Madison nodded her head.

"No, not easy at all," responded Regan. "But I think our relationship is making it even more difficult," she stated calmly.

"What do you mean?" asked Madison, with a quizzical look.

"Well," said Regan, "I think what's happening is that you two are not demonstrating trust in me through your actions."

"Trust?" Madison said, taken aback. "We trust you implicitly. That's why we chose you for the job."

"I know you *think* you trust me," said Regan. "But I believe you're having some trouble *actually* trusting me."

"OK, we're listening," said Madison seriously.

"Here's an example," Regan shared. "In bringing together two companies, it's important to make sure everyone is working from the same set of facts. When we were smaller, we used to rely on daily reports from supervisors to ensure everything was on schedule. But now that we're responsible for so much more, we need to stay more on top of project status and identify problems sooner. So I implemented a new computer system for the executive team, which you vetted and approved, that allows us to track the increased volume we're producing."

Regan continued, "The new software required the executive team to attend a series of training sessions, which you also approved. But when you two heard that two members of the executive team were worried about the time the training would take away from their regular responsibilities, you had me cancel the training sessions and delay the rollout of the new system."

"That's right," Madison confirmed. "After considering it, we thought with everything else going on that it would be better to delay implementing a new computer system until after everyone got a better handle on things."

"I understand that concern," said Regan, "but there were several reasons why I decided to time it that way." She explained, "First, while there was a lot going on with the merger, I still wanted to rip this particular bandage off right away. It's a big deal to introduce or change computer systems, and I didn't want anyone getting used to an old system and then soon after have to learn a whole new one.

"Second, any time a company merges, customers become concerned that the transition will delay their products and deliverables. And keeping track of all the new volume we're producing is a huge task. I wanted our executives to have all the necessary information at their fingertips from day one, to make sure no customer felt a negative impact from our merger.

"Third, the training sessions weren't just for 'training.' They were also a way to get all the executives in the same room, getting to know each other better and building camaraderie. It's like preseason training for a sports team. Sharing the same experience is a great way to bond. We were also going to have coffee breaks and after-training happy hours. Nothing can replicate the team building that happens by spending time together.

"And finally, having me cancel the rollout of one of my first big initiatives made me look weak to the executive team. All one of them had to do was complain over my head, and they got their way. I can't hold the team to task if they don't think you'll back me up," Regan concluded.

"I see. I didn't know that," admitted Luke. "And so by having you delay the computer system, Madison and I put your goals in danger and undercut your authority."

"I know you didn't do it on purpose," Regan said. "But when you change your mind on something you've already approved, or give in to employee desires without consulting me, it puts me in a difficult spot. I know you love this company, and I know it's hard to step away from things you've been able to control successfully for years. But part of the point of making me president was so you two didn't have to spend the time on those decisions anymore, so you could focus on the larger vision. I really believe in that vision, but to help you achieve it, you have to let me do my job," Regan reminded them.

Luke and Madison considered what Regan told them. They recognized their behavior in her words and understood they had made her already-difficult job even more challenging. In their next meeting with Regan, Luke and Madison vowed to do better. They no longer made decisions impacting employees without consulting with her first. They stopped nitpicking her every move and gave her new initiatives a fair chance. Luke and Madison made a showing of support for Regan by personally promoting the new computer system, preparing employees for the transition, and even attending the training sessions themselves.

Just as Brady and his coach operate, Regan returned their trust in her with her own trust in them. She was careful to keep Luke and Madison fully in the loop on her decision-making process, was transparent in her procedures, and listened carefully to their advice. With improved openness and trust, the relationship between Luke, Madison, and Regan grew into a powerful alliance that brought the company to the next level. The company achieved its annual goals, made measurable progress towards its ultimate vision, and became a leader in the industry.

MORE ACTION FROM THE BUSINESS STADIUM: LESS INFORMATION MEANS LESS TRUST

Trusting your colleagues does not require you to be best friends with each member of your team. It's safe to assume that Brady is closer with some teammates than he is with others. Brady knows, however, that he needs to give respect to and receive respect from every teammate. Luke, Madison, and Regan had the advantage of a history of a strong relationship, but that's not the case in every company. Creating an atmosphere where coworkers have respect for one another requires time and effort.

An IT consulting company was experiencing personal discord among some of its top executives. Logan, the CEO, hired a business coach, Henry, to help build better relationships among the leadership team. Logan described to Henry the tension that he often felt from certain executives and explained the energy in the C-suite seemed to be devolving into something very negative. Logan explained that he really tried to support his executives and worked to create opportunities for the team to build camaraderie, but his efforts seemed to fail at every turn. Logan was concerned this could spoil the team approach he was trying to create, and could even bleed into other areas of the company.

Henry took to Logan immediately. Henry saw a leader who wanted what was best for his team and was willing to sacrifice on its behalf. Logan seemed genuinely concerned that he had alienated some executives. Henry knew from past experience that plenty of leaders didn't even notice if their employees didn't like them, so he appreciated that Logan both noticed and cared. Henry sensed that Logan had the right stuff to be a great leader, but just needed a little refinement.

Wanting more information, Henry set up a meeting with Logan and his top manager, Noah. The day before the meeting, Logan asked to reschedule, and Henry had no problem making the adjustment. He asked Noah if they could have a one-on-one meeting instead. Henry could tell Noah was bothered by something, but Noah still agreed to the appointment.

The next day, the meeting between Henry and Noah immediately uncovered drama.

"Man, that was some kind of move Logan pulled yesterday, huh?" asked Noah, clearly annoyed. He went on, "I mean, he sets up this meeting with an outside consultant, everyone's all set to go, and then at the last minute, he cancels. Classic."

Henry was surprised at Noah's strong reaction to what seemed to Henry a minor, understandable schedule adjustment. Henry was also taken aback that a member of his team could dislike Logan so much, when Logan seemed so supportive.

Henry wanted to know why, so he neutrally asked Noah, "Did that mess your schedule up?"

Noah considered for a second, and then responded, "Well, really, no. It wasn't a big deal, at least this time. But Logan does this kind of stuff all the time. He's constantly rearranging scheduled meetings. Something always comes up and he just changes willy-nilly. He doesn't care whether it messes up your schedule, or who needed to move other meetings to be available during the original time he requested, or how anyone has to bend over backwards to make the rescheduled event. I don't know if he doesn't take us seriously or just doesn't care or what. But I can never reliably plan my day, and it makes me look like an idiot in front of my team when he doesn't show at the last minute."

Henry felt disappointed. Had he misjudged Logan? After years of successful business coaching, were Henry's instincts failing him? Henry knew that leaders needed to be reliable. Tom

Brady would never miss an offensive unit meeting. As he was about to depart the office, Henry met another executive, Allison. She agreed to a quick preliminary discussion about the office atmosphere. Henry began gently, commenting that he'd heard from other executives that scheduling was often a problem.

"I mean, yeah, sometimes," Allison responded. She continued, "Logan does change his schedule around a lot, sometimes without much warning. But it's always with good reason. He's really great about helping the executives and front-line employees when they need it. When a team falls behind, he can deliver a motivational speech or show support for a team leader who's trying to get everyone on schedule. If there's trouble with a sale, he's always willing to make time to reassure the client that they're a priority. It makes a big difference."

"So if it's always to support another executive, why do you think some executives have such a strong reaction to his scheduling changes?" Henry queried.

Allison sighed. "It's a couple of things. For one, Logan doesn't always communicate well. He just says he has to change the meeting, but doesn't usually say why. I only know because I'm friendly with his executive assistant and with some of the team leaders he's supported. His intention is good, but it often comes off badly when he doesn't explain.

"And then when Logan does change things, some of the executives get super annoyed. A couple of them have such bad attitudes that it infects the rest of the team. They're good at their jobs, but their negativity bleeds into everything else. It's caused rifts between Logan and some of the executives, and among some of the executives as well. For being an executive team, we're not much of a 'team.' It all starts pretty minor, but it really snowballs," Allison concluded.

Over the next few weeks, Henry had similar conversations with other executives. They appreciated Logan's willingness to help, but couldn't understand his sudden disappearances, and it bred distrust among the executive team. Henry was relieved his impression of Logan wasn't far off the mark.

Logan had the best intentions, but was simply failing to communicate well. Brady's thorough communication built trust with his team, while Logan's poor communication damaged trust with his. Henry scheduled a meeting with Logan to share his findings.

"Logan, I've had some really interesting conversations with your executive team," Henry began. "It seems like you've really made an effort to do all you can to eliminate obstacles for your team. They've noticed, and they appreciate it."

"That's good!" Logan responded.

Henry hesitated.

"Well, it's good and bad," he began. "They like that you take their concerns seriously and are willing to help. But they have trouble dealing with your frequent schedule changes. It makes them feel like you don't respect their time. And when you don't give a clear reason why you've rescheduled, it can come off as rude and disrespectful."

"Oh, no," replied Logan. "That's not at all what I intended. It's just that I don't want to make an executive feel like they look bad in front of their colleagues because they needed help from the boss. I'm actually trying to demonstrate how much I *do* respect them."

Henry's interest was piqued.

"So when your executives ask for your help, do you think they should be embarrassed?" asked Henry.

"No, not at all. My team is really good. They impress me all the time with what they're able to accomplish. Lots of times the problem isn't even their fault. Besides, everyone needs support now and again," Logan asserted.

"I see what you're trying to do, Logan," Henry said. "But I think you're actually communicating the opposite of what you intend. By hiding the support you're giving one executive, you're demonstrating to him that he's done something wrong, something to be ashamed of. You're also implying that the other executives won't be able to tell the difference between a good and bad executive.

"It all comes off like you don't trust them. And in return, some of them don't trust you, especially when they feel like you blow off their meetings without justification. It sounds like you actually do trust your team, but you need to communicate that message to them clearly. Say it and demonstrate it. Otherwise they'll never stop infighting, and never become a real team."

Logan took Henry's words to heart. He tried harder to stick to his schedule. When he did have to miss meetings, he shared the reasons. To Logan's surprise, the executives impacted hardly ever minded, even those who had previously been the most sensitive to the changes. Further, the executives who needed help overcame any embarrassment and actually had more to contribute in leadership team meetings about how other executives might avoid the same pitfalls.

As in Brady's film reviews, the team members started learning from one another's mistakes and sharing best practices. The executives became more open with one another and more collaborative. The internal drama that had plagued the team decreased. Not all the executives loved each other, and some of them still weren't buddy-buddy with Logan, but once Logan started demonstrating his trust in and respect for them by communicating more information, everyone was better able to work together. Like Brady strives for on his teams, Logan's team members respected one another, and together, Logan and the executive team grew the company into a leader in IT consulting.

GAME REVIEW:

- It's one thing to build trust, and another thing to maintain it. Even longtime, historically strong working relationships require ongoing effort. Don't take them for granted. Nurture them and continue investing in their success.

(Continued on next page)

- Leaders need to leave their own baggage behind, and shouldn't let it interfere with how they operate. Simultaneously, they need to understand that their team members may be burdened by old baggage that impacts their work and relationships. Leaders should seek to recognize and eliminate these roadblocks by working to build trust.
- Sharing information is a fundamental part of building trust within teams. It demonstrates a leader's belief in the team and helps ensure the members of the team are all working from the same set of facts.
- Don't assume others understand your subtleties. Communicate clearly and explicitly with words and back them up with consistent action.

COMMUNICATING TRUST

Brady, Regan, and Henry know that productive communication in the workplace requires trust and respect. Baggage from the past may cause people to assume their colleagues don't have the right intentions, but one should not give in to this impulse. You may not be able to change people, but you can change your reactions to them and end the negative cycle of behavior. Instead of allowing problems to fester, leaders should look to resolve conflict proactively. You do not have to be best friends, but you do have to respect each other.

To take hold, the behavior of trust needs to start at the top. Some leaders struggle with trust because it requires an inherent vulnerability, which they may not like to reveal. Brady demonstrates vulnerability by admitting his own mistakes. Trust means relying on the other person to listen and consider carefully, instead of rushing to judgment or ridicule. Brady demonstrates that respect to his teammates and expects the same in return. Employees depend on leaders to follow through on their word and not to change their minds without cause. They, in turn, depend on leaders for the same respect and support. If leaders don't demonstrate trust in their employees, employees will have a much harder time trusting their leaders.

There are several ways leaders can build trust. Many choose to speak last during meetings, not first. It's important to let ideas flow or grievances air before shutting down debate. Employees need to feel heard and appreciated, just as Brady listens carefully to his teammates. This may require leaders to pull some team members out of their shell. Other leaders work to become comfortable with quiet pauses in their meetings. Don't feel the need to fill every moment with talking. It's OK to give attendees a moment to process the information they're receiving and consider its consequences. Leaders should also remember that silence does not necessarily mean acquiescence. Further, don't let assent from a few speak for the whole group. Those who lead meetings must toe the line between avoiding unnecessary or redundant debate and ensuring that everyone participates.

Another way leaders can build trust is through consistency. Brady is a paradigm of consistent routine. What employees see is what they should get. If leaders say they will take some action, they need to follow through on that promise. Further, leaders should develop regular processes that encourage their teams to speak up, share ideas, engage in debate, and support one another. This can be achieved through a regular, efficient meeting structure (like those described in Chapter 2); regular company-wide communication from leadership; and follow-through on promises. Brady's film sessions are consistent in structure, tone, and emotion.

Finally, transparency from leaders proves to employees that actions match words. You can demonstrate this by showing full openness on financial decisions, by taking responsibility for your own failings, and by holding leadership accountable when they make a mistake. Here again, regular company-wide communication is an important method of maintaining open lines of communication. Brady always takes ownership of his missteps, whether it's in a game or in practice, and does so privately as well as to the press.

Once you build trust, each communication between leaders and employees can be productive. If everything is working smoothly, leadership has an opportunity to congratulate and reward the team and find ways to be even more efficient. They can avert problems before they even come about. Trust is an important reason why Brady, despite a constantly changing roster around him, has been able to lead his team to such sustained success.

EXECUTING THE PLAY

Exercises for the Preseason:

- The next time you reprimand a team member, carefully evaluate your response. What happened that led to the misstep? Could your own poor communication, inadequate instructions, or decision not to share all relevant information have contributed? Have your words and actions demonstrated that you will be able to trust them the next time a similar situation arises?

- Consider instituting full transparency on company finances. It can help employees understand exactly the role they play and what their performance means to the company's bottom line. For more information, read Jack Stack's book *The Great Game of Business*, about open-book management.

Best Practices for the Game:

- Be crystal clear in communication with colleagues. Don't leave any room for misinterpretation. For example, before you send an email, read it from the recipient's point of view, and consider how that person might receive the message.

- Share information as much as possible. Besides daily huddles with your team, have regular company-wide meetings

where you communicate priorities, remind employees of company goals, and point out strong performances.
- Always take full responsibility for your mistakes. Even the most successful leaders make them. Instead of avoiding or deflecting blame, look for ways to proactively solve the problem, and welcome input from your team.

CHAPTER 8

Elevate Everyone

"My connection with [my team] is through joy and love. It's not through fear or insults. That's not how I lead. When you have a group of people who hold each other accountable every day, those are the teammates that you're looking for."[1]
—Tom Brady

INTERCEPTING A MESSAGE

Pretend you are a rookie defensive back on the practice squad of the Tampa Bay Buccaneers. You had a respectable college career, but as expected, you went undrafted after graduation. Still, you were invited to a Buccaneers tryout. Although they cut you from the regular 53-man roster, they immediately signed you to the practice squad, the 10-player unit used during practices to mimic the next game's opponent and prepare the team. You've tried to make the most of the opportunity, working hard in the weight room, on the field, and in the film room. Now that you've had a few months with the Bucs both your physical frame and your decision-making on the field make you look less like a rookie and more like a veteran.

Guys make the jump from practice squad to roster spot all the time. Even some great players such as Danny Amendola, James Harrison, and Arian Foster started as practice squad players.[2] You're on a mission to exceed expectations just like they did. You plan to play so well that the head coach has no choice but to sign you to the team.

One morning, you show up at the facility ready to work. Per NFL rules, the team generally is only allowed one full-contact padded practice per week,[3] so it's the most important day of the week for you to show what you've got. A high-performing practice squad helps your team win on Sunday, and all the coaches watch. The team you're going up against this week is known for stout defense, and particularly for the skill of its secondary, charged with shutting down Brady's pass opportunities. As a cornerback, a position typically assigned to cover wide receivers, it's your time to shine.

You don your pads and helmet, then warm up with the team. As the full squad scrimmage begins, you're laser focused. After a few downs, the ball hasn't come to your side of the field. Suddenly you think you recognize the way Brady has the offense lined up pre-snap. You've seen this in your film study, and you know how the play is going to develop. If it's what you think, you need to change your ultimate position on the field. You carefully watch to see if the offense gives away anything else, but they reveal nothing.

The center snaps the ball, and Brady drops back as you backpedal into position. You pretend you're following the wide receiver and stay on him tightly at first, watching Brady at the same time. You see Brady's eyes move as he reads through his progressions to determine the best option, and you know it's the play you suspected. As Brady scans the field, you ease off the wide receiver you've been covering, knowing your teammate will pick him up. Instead, you locate the slot receiver, who lined up between the offensive line of scrimmage and your wide receiver. You start shifting over to him, knowing that in a few moments, Brady will find him open and throw him the ball.

Once you see Brady register the fact that his target is open, you break towards the receiver at full speed. You've timed your run perfectly. As Brady starts his throwing motion, you're already blazing towards the spot he'll deliver the pass. You can tell you'll have an angle on the ball. You could intercept it. You could intercept Tom Brady! But that also means . . . you might intercept Tom Brady.

You've heard horror stories from other teams of quarterbacks flipping out on practice squad players who intercept them. Sometimes even their coaches get involved and quietly ask the practice squad to go a little easy on the quarterback.[4] No one with this team has ever asked you to do something like that. But you have seen Brady go off before in practice, demanding performance from his teammates or getting in a shouting match with an assistant coach. It's not pretty. And if you're trying to make the regular roster, the last thing you need is for coaches to see Brady screaming at you.

You have to make a split-second decision. You can make the right defensive play and break up the pass, but risk the wrath of Brady and maybe your potential spot on the team. Or you can let the ball go, which is likely how most defensive backs would play it since they probably wouldn't notice something so subtle in their film study. You'd give up an understandable reception and keep the peace with Brady and the coaches. It's a tempting option.

Competitive instinct and pride take over; you're not going to miss your chance to prove yourself. Without breaking stride, you extend your arms and snatch the ball right out of the air, getting it firmly under your control before the intended receiver even realizes what's happening. You run down the field and try to find some blockers to get as much yardage as possible. Eventually you're tackled, but you've made a nice run.

As you get up from the bottom of the pile, you look for Brady. He's livid. Even from a distance, you can see he's red in the face and can hear the expletives coming out of his mouth. He doesn't direct anything towards you, or even look at you, but that doesn't mean he's not furious about what you've done. Coaches are taking notes. For the remainder of the scrimmage, the ball doesn't come your direction again, and you don't know if that's good or bad.

Finally, practice is over, and you quietly make your way to the locker room, still unsure of what might happen. It's crowded, and you're relieved not to see Brady anywhere nearby. You shower and gather your things to go home. But just as you're turning around to leave, you see Brady walking towards your locker. Fight or flight? You're just not sure, so you stand perfectly still, as if you're hoping a bear won't see you.

As he gets closer, Brady reaches for his wallet. He stops right in front of you, pulls out several bills, and holds them out towards you. Stunned, you just stand there. Brady waits until you finally reach out and take the money. He looks you right in the eyes as he tells you to keep it up, then turns and walks away.

The player at the next locker sees your perplexed expression and laughs.

"First time, huh?" he asks.

"What?" you respond after a pause, bewildered.

"First time you've intercepted Brady. He always pays the practice squad guys who pick him off," your teammate replies, as if this is common knowledge. [5]

"Wait, why? Isn't he pissed?" you question.

"Maybe," your teammates says, "but at himself, not at you. The money is motivation and reward. He wants everyone to *bring it* at practice, every play, and he notices when they do. Good job," he concludes.

Although you're still shocked, you feel an immediate mental shift.

A superstar quarterback just paid you cold, hard cash for making him look bad, in public no less. Who does that? Brady's reaction tells you beyond doubt what his priorities are: this man wants to *win*. He doesn't care who you are or what pedigree you have; he just cares if you can play.

If getting humbled by a member of the scout team is what it takes to improve, Brady is ready to embrace it. And when he paid you in the middle of a crowded locker room, you recognized he was telling his teammates they better be willing to undergo the same.

Another thing strikes you, too. Some stars don't like it when others take away from their spotlight. Brady, however, doesn't mind pointing out excellent performance wherever he sees it. In fact, he seems to like it. He wasn't upset when he gave you the money. He was smiling! You won't forget this moment or his message any time soon.

After this, you're not worried anymore about how starters will react if you make a nice play against them. Football is no place for shyness or taking it easy. Your job is to prepare the team for the opponent, who certainly won't take it easy. And if you want to be on the regular roster, intercepting Brady is exactly what could get you there. For the remainder of the season, you play fearless defense in practice. Coaches take notice, and later in the season you even intercept Brady again and pocket more of his cash. You feel more confident than ever that next season, you'll earn the roster spot you've dreamed of.

LEADERSHIP LESSONS FROM THE FIELD:

- Great leaders find compelling ways to communicate with their team. Leaders present critical information in a way that will get in their teams' heads and stay there.
- Reward hard work and smart moves. The best leaders aren't afraid of being outshined by a member of their team—in fact, they like it.
- Leaders celebrate the achievements of others, even if it comes at their own expense.
- Effective leaders take full responsibility for their own mistakes. They never deflect blame to those above or below.

ENCOURAGE THIRD-STRING SUPERSTARS

Tom Brady is a master at pushing himself to his limits. Still, there are plenty of players in the NFL who work hard, so it takes more than that to reach a championship level. What sets Brady apart is the way he's able to elicit the best from others as well. Athletes and businesspeople alike need reminders to stay at the top of their games and maintain high levels of motivation.

Great leaders help people perform better, inspiring growth by setting a strong example and highlighting the excellence of others. Brady's behavior demonstrates an unwavering commitment to achieving peak performance, from his daily routine, to his eating habits, to his hours of mental preparation. His teammates take notice of his approach and work to become more like him. His teammates also reap rewards from Brady, whether it's cash for an interception or a shoutout in a film review meeting for a smart play.

Leaders should express gratitude to teammates who do good work and motivate them to keep improving. An effective form of motivation is public recognition of a job well done. Leaders need to acknowledge all the contributions from their team. It doesn't matter if the contributor's role is small. Like the cornerback in the story above, the contribution can even be seemingly contradictory: interceptions are bad for an offense, but having them in practice leaves the team time to correct errors. Without excellent performance from others, team success is that much harder to achieve.

The best leaders understand that one person alone can't create a healthy culture.[6] No matter how good an idea, leaders need buy in from others to bring it to life. Great leaders know that "follow-ship" can, in fact, be the highest form of leadership. It may sound counterintuitive, but it's a critical skill. A leader who's also a good follower can recognize someone else's good idea, and even give up control of a project to the person best suited to lead it. An effective leader sacrifices individual glory to share the limelight, which ultimately adds to the overall brightness of victory.

The core of great leadership is manipulating people—yes, manipulating, but in a good way!—to do what you want them to do, in a way that makes them feel happy and excited to do it. Brady's strong example and willingness to elevate those around him turn his team into a cohesive force that effectively fights battles and ultimately wins wars.

ACTION FROM THE BUSINESS STADIUM: HITTING A LEADERSHIP CEILING

A clothing manufacturing company purchased a smaller competitor. Brian, the CEO, was particularly excited about absorbing the competitor because it had a strong, longtime client relationship with a large department store. The COO, Maria, had never overseen a merger before, but she was looking forward to the challenge and to the fresh personalities and ideas the new team would infuse into the now-larger company. Brian and Maria kept their longtime vice president of production, Avery, and brought in the smaller company's vice president of marketing, Vince.

The four executives organized a company-wide town hall. The goal of the event was to introduce all the employees and executives, start building team camaraderie, and explain how the new company would function. Brady always ensures similar training to familiarize new teammates with the way things work. After working with Brian for several years, Maria and Avery knew he was a terrific speaker and very motivating. Unfortunately, he also tended to shoot from the hip and occasionally even made inappropriate comments. He insisted on emceeing the event, so they encouraged him to write the script in advance so they could give feedback, even though he often balked at critique.

Brian's initial proposed script mentioned the sales team, but never specifically welcomed any other division of the company.

The text was enthusiastic but somewhat aggressive and overall left the other three executives somewhat cold.

"Brian, I love the energy in the script. Your excitement clearly comes through, and it will enliven the town hall and make the employees eager to get going," said Maria. "I do think you should name the operations, marketing, and production teams just as you do the sales team. We want to make sure everyone feels welcomed and recognized."

"Oh, yeah, I guess you're right," commented Brian. "I just get really amped about sales because they're most important." Unlike Brady, Brian didn't always appreciate the important role each member of the team played.

"Well, they are very important, of course, but we need the other divisions to make sure the sales team has something to sell!" Avery reminded.

"I'd also like to have a meeting with just the sales team after the town hall. I want to familiarize new members with our sales playbook and our existing clients, and I want to give them a real motivational talk. I want to get this thing off to a running start!" exclaimed Brian.

"You can certainly do that," said a wary Avery, "but if you do, I suggest you have meetings with each of the other divisions, too. We don't want them to feel unimportant, especially as we're welcoming new people and trying to make the transition seamless."

"Yeah OK that's fine. I won't need as long with the others," he agreed.

"And Brian, I'd like to suggest after your speech that you field questions from the audience. It would be a nice personal touch, and employees always appreciate the ability to ask questions straight to the top," said Avery.

"Mmm, good idea," Brian commented. "So Maria, you're organizing the town hall and you'll finalize this script for me. Is there anything else you need from me or are we done here?" said Brian, already nearly out of his chair.

"Brian, I'd like to discuss our marketing approach to the department store client. I know you want to get moving on that, so I'd like to share some insights from our past experience with them," offered Vince.

"I'm actually about to get on a call with them right now. Can we talk after?" asked Brian, ushering the executives out of his office.

"Oh, sure, that's fine. Just let me know when you're ready," responded Vince.

When Brian shut his door to get on the call, Maria, Avery, and Vince had a brief chat.

"Maria, is there anything we can do to help with the town hall?" asked Vince.

"I don't think so. Just have to keep an eye out for my new version of Brian's script. Vince, you looked a little apprehensive when Brian said he was about to get on the phone with the department store," Maria commented.

"Yeah, the department store is a little tricky sometimes, and they're used to things a particular way. But Brian is a master salesman. Everybody in the sector knows him. I'm sure it will be OK," Vince assured.

When the day of the town hall arrived, Brian was in his element. He was highly charismatic and commanded the audience. Unfortunately, true to Maria and Avery's fears, he did go off script. He mentioned the other departments, but lost some of the passion he displayed when he spoke about sales. During the question and answer session, he made a fat joke about a popular mid-level manager. The manager and tenured employees laughed, knowing that the manager had a great sense of humor and understanding Brian's tendency to perform off the cuff. However, it made the new employees very uncomfortable and made Brian come off as mean-spirited. Overall, the town hall was a success, but Brian's performance left something to be desired.

At the division breakout sessions after the town hall, Brian's conduct again generated mixed reactions. With the sales team, he was hard-driving and inspiring. Based on his presentation and his answers to questions, he was determined to keep the sales process the same, without incorporating anything from the new employees. Brian's existing sales process was strong, but it was a missed opportunity to recognize new employees and possibly enhance the sales process.

During the breakout sessions with the marketing and production teams, he lacked spirit. He was encouraging of the marketing team, but clearly viewed it as a subordinate to sales. Every answer he gave focused on what it meant to the sales team. Vince was disappointed Brian seemed to feel that marketing was inferior to sales, instead of a capable, independent group that could generate real value for the company and its customers.

When it came to operations, Brian was downright dismissive. He only carved out a short span of time, rushed through his remarks, and ended the session as soon as he could. His message was one of warning against mistakes, rather than encouraging a job well done. It was an error Brady never makes. While he carefully reviews film with his teammates and points out their missteps, he does it to give them tools to improve their play, not to intimidate them. Although she expected this attitude from Brian, Maria was still disheartened and apprehensive about how her team would react.

After the town hall, and as the new and old teams continued to combine, Vince and Avery were disconcerted by Brian's behavior. They were unsure how to reassure their teams that leadership supported them. They were also put off by how some of Brian's decisions were negatively impacting the transition for new employees and clients. Maria was Brian's most trusted colleague, so they set a meeting with her to discuss how to approach the issues.

"I know how Brian comes off," commiserated Maria. "But he's great at sales and makes a ton of money for the company. He's not going anywhere. We're going to have to take the good with the bad with him." In a way, it was like Brady defending Belichick, understanding his measures were extreme, but appreciating the results.

"I know he's a good salesman, but I'm actually concerned about the impact he's having on future sales," said Vince. "The marketing people that came with me from the other company are really surprised by some of his moves. Remember when he had that phone call with the department store after our town hall planning meeting? From what I understand from my contacts there, he basically told them all the things that were going to change, as if they were all good things. But like I said, they can be finicky on certain things, and they felt like he didn't give them a chance to explain."

"There's more," offered Avery. "One of the things he promised the department store was faster delivery after sale. But he never consulted with me how that would impact the factory. He just assumed we'd be able to do it right away. It's not that easy. We didn't have the new team fully trained on the machines, and we had to wait for delivery of a fabric we'd never used before. We just weren't ready to launch into full production. As a result, a lot of the tenured guys had to pull extra shifts or babysit new employees who hadn't finished training."

"The other thing is, based on my experience with the department store, they don't actually care that much about delivery speed," added Vince. "They care a lot more about customer service and collaboration. Part of the reason why the old company had such a longstanding relationship with them was because we were willing to work so closely with them, experiment with different fabrics and designs, meet their special requests. The new marketing and sales people tried to tell Brian, but he never listened."

Maria absorbed what Avery and Vince told her, and promised she would consider what to do. She also decided to ask their thoughts on another topic.

"By the way, I've been thinking about the town hall we had. I thought it was reasonably successful, despite Brian's shortcomings, and I wondered what you two thought about making them a quarterly event," Maria suggested.

"I think that's a terrific idea. We had them all the time at the old company, and it was a great opportunity to remind everyone of the bigger picture, build trust with leadership, and keep a human connection between divisions," asserted Vince.

"I agree," said Avery. "I'm totally on board."

"Great. I think we should build up to them, so we get a hang of the rhythm of a large meeting. I'd like to propose that the three of us each emcee monthly meetings with our divisions. We'll get used to planning and organizing these events, so that by the time of the next quarterly, we'll be well versed and it won't require as much last-minute planning as last time," Maria said.

Avery and Vince enthusiastically jumped into planning their meetings. Maria was delighted to see the energy they brought to make the events useful, interesting, and fun for their teams. To support her executives and demonstrate leadership buy-in to attendees, Maria attended each division's monthly meeting. She was particularly impressed by Vince. He clearly had a knack for large corporate events: he anticipated audience needs, understood how to prepare presenters, and was natural on stage. His audience left the presentation with a better understanding of their important role in the company and a renewed belief in their mission.

Maria knew she had to do something to rein in Brian, and she had an idea for town halls moving forward. She scheduled a meeting and told him she felt some apprehension about the progress of the transition.

"Are we going to have one of these meetings again?" demanded Brian. "You're constantly telling me what I'm doing wrong."

"I know feedback can be difficult to hear. I don't like it either!" she sympathized. "Still, I need to bring these things to your attention. We're on the verge of something great at this company, but nobody's perfect. It's a hard process."

"Yeah, yeah," Brian dismissed. "So what's the problem this time?"

"It seems you're forcing through some sales changes that are causing challenges for other divisions in the company. You didn't do it intentionally, of course, but we need to find a way to produce the sales results you want while causing less disruption internally," Maria said. She described to him the complications in marketing and manufacturing.

"Look, Maria, I've got a mandate from the board to increase revenue, expand our client base, and grow this company. I can't do that without demanding some changes in sales. That's my strength. I know what needs to be done," he asserted.

"No one's arguing your sales instincts. You're the best. What I'm suggesting is that you operate more collaboratively with your executives, instead of just demanding immediate changes. We can still implement what you want, we just need to do it in a way that allows managers to anticipate challenges and advocate for their teams. Lots of the problems I told you about were avoidable, if they'd just had a little warning," Maria said.

Brian sighed.

"I'd also like to discuss our plan for regular town halls," Maria continued. "I've been watching Vince interact with his team and conduct his monthly division meetings. Brian, he's really good. He's got presence on stage. He's got charm and humor, he's uplifting—I can't say enough about his performance. Also, you and I have seen her in action, and we already know that Avery is great with an audience. I'd like to nominate them to emcee our town halls going forward," stated Maria.

"Instead of me?" asked Brian, surprised. "But I'm great on stage!"

"You are, but hear me out. By allowing Avery and Vince to do it, you're accomplishing other objectives. First, you're highlighting the role of a new guy, which will make the other new team members feel included and comfortable. Second, you're allowing everyone to hear new voices. That's a good think on its own, plus it will keep your voice fresh and motivating, and make your voice carry even more weight for the most important items. And you're letting others shine, without suffering any decrease in quality, which demonstrates your ability to recognize others' skills and reward them for it. It's a great move," concluded Maria.

Brian thought for a few moments, then said, "OK, I see your point. Avery and Vince can do the town halls. Now, regarding the sales stuff, I can't make any promises. But I will at least consider what you've told me."

Maria left her meeting with Brian feeling better than she expected. People like Brian do not change overnight, but she hoped his willingness to listen was a positive sign. She understood Brian's strengths and weaknesses, and worked to shield others from the negative impacts of his weaknesses. Maria was also encouraged by the more prominent role Vince would play. She knew that advocating for and empowering her people was among her most important responsibilities. It built morale, encouraged team members, and produced great ideas. Like Brady, Maria set a positive example in her interactions with employees at every level and encouraged other leaders like Brian to do the same, even when it didn't come naturally to them.

GAME REVIEW:

- Effective leaders never belittle others, on matters personal or professional. It damages morale everywhere. It also makes them seem like an enemy who cannot be approached for help or trusted as reliable.
- Great leaders listen. And they don't just listen when others are talking directly to them. They listen all the time, hear what others *aren't* saying, and read the behavior of others. They then act to solve problems and support their teams.
- The best leaders don't hide from criticism: they put their egos aside and actively seek feedback. They are always looking for ways to improve and be more useful to their teams.

EXECUTING THE PLAY

Exercises for the Preseason:

- How do you recognize great performances by those on your team? Do you look for them, track them, and make a point of sharing those achievements with others? When you do share these moments, what impact does it have on team morale?

- Think about the last time you had to discipline or take to task a member of your team. Had you been the guilty party, who would have held you accountable? *Would* someone have held you accountable? The last time you made a mistake, did you acknowledge it to your team, publicly holding yourself to the same standards you hold them?

- The more people you elevate, the more you will get out of each one, and the deeper their engagement will be. Consider new ways you might give others opportunities to prove themselves beyond their existing abilities. Plan to help them shine, while also allowing them to fail safely.

Best Practices for the Game:

- Institute an official system for seeking feedback from your teammates and those subordinate to you. It will teach your team how to give constructive criticism and make them more comfortable seeking feedback for themselves.

- When you contribute to a problem, own up to your mistakes, even if it was only a minor cause. Effective leaders understand that teams succeed or fail together, and that every individual plays an important role.

- Highlight impressive performances by members of your team. Public recognition is a meaningful reward, and it offers examples to others of how they can improve.

CHAPTER 9

Talk to People Where They Are

*"You take the learning when it comes, but it's a constant process.
It happens in the meetings, happens in the walk-throughs, and
happens in the games."*[1]
—Tom Brady

TOM THE STORYTELLING TECHIE

Michael Jordan, perhaps the greatest basketball player of all time, didn't make his high school's varsity team as a sophomore.[2] Tom Brady, perhaps the greatest quarterback of all time, was the backup quarterback on his high school's winless freshman team in 1991. Both men used these and other wounds to fuel their incredible competitive fire. They found the motivation they needed in the stories from their past. It was likely one of the first times each understood the power of compelling storytelling to drive behavior.

Several years later, Brady again learned the power of storytelling, this time in a public context. In early 2011, Brady was practically on top of the world. He already had more success in his career than most achieve in a lifetime, including three Super Bowl championships. In the 2010 season, the Patriots captured another AFC East Division title, won 14 games, and had eight players selected to the Pro Bowl.[3] Brady had another prolific season in which he threw for 3,900 yards with only four interceptions.[4] He was named NFL MVP and Offensive

Player of the year.[5] He had two children and was married to a supermodel.[6] To the average American, Brady had exactly zero reason to be upset about anything in his life.

Professional athletes are hero worshipped in this country, assumed to be fierce warriors who never reveal weakness, and Brady is among the most famous and successful of all time. Which is why seeing Brady cry in an interview on national television was so remarkable to much of the public. In an ESPN documentary, Brady recounted his experience in the 2000 NFL Draft,[7] in which he wasn't taken until the sixth round, pick number 199, the seventh quarterback selected.[8] As he shared the story of watching the draft at home with his family, walking around the block while waiting in agony, Brady became obviously choked up, emotions pouring out of him.

The video clip was an instant sensation. Some felt bad for Brady, who was clearly still so hurt and embarrassed by his precipitous drop in the draft. Many felt his emotion was the mark of a true champion, someone never satisfied and always looking to prove doubters wrong. Others mocked Brady for being a crybaby, particularly when he found so much success after the draft. The reactions varied across the spectrum, but either way, there were a *ton* of reactions. It's still regularly brought up every year around draft time or when Brady does well in the postseason.

The huge public discussion about that interview was no doubt in Brady's mind a couple years later when he wanted to start building his TB12 brand. Social media was exploding, and Brady likely saw it as an excellent opportunity to promote his health and lifestyle company. Brady was sure to get attention as a celebrity sports figure, but there are lots of celebrities on social media. How could Brady's account stand out, particularly beyond just New England fans, and develop a real following?

To grow his personal following, Brady uses a variety of multimedia tools, authenticity, and storytelling that creates an emotional connection with his audience. Brady's first social media account was Facebook. He uses that platform to share pieces of his family life, offseason activities, postgame wrap-ups, and more, with pictures, videos, and graphics. Some of it is inspirational, some demonstrates his absolute devotion to football, and some is downright funny, like the picture he shared of his college résumé.[9] Brady seamlessly integrates branded content into his feed, like when he posted a picture of himself in a helmet, laying on a sponsor company's mattress at the top of a flight of stairs, explaining that he needed to get his body prepared for the collisions he would absorb in preseason.[10] He makes it topical and even a little meta, like when he parodied college athletic recruitment announcements by teasing and later broadcasting on Facebook Live his selection of his next social media account (it was Instagram, by the way).[11]

Now, Brady's not sweating the details of his next social media post. He has a team that manages it for him.[12] Still, Brady understands the important role social media can play and sees the opportunity for growing his brand and spreading inspiration. Plus, he's smart enough to know that it's a good idea to hire other people who are talented in the specific ways necessary to get the most out of social media. It's just another example of his personal discipline.

So when Brady was ready to take his TB12 brand national, he used a similar approach. He regularly incorporated TB12 into his social media feeds, sometimes subtly with apparel and sometimes more directly with links to special sales. The biggest move of all was his decision to create *Tom vs Time*,[13] a documentary about his process that would air on Facebook. The series provides an in-depth look at how Brady lives his life and balances football and family, including a great deal of information about his TB12 method and his claims about its transformative power.

By all accounts, the campaign was a success. *Tom vs Time* got more than 50 million views; two-thirds of the audience didn't follow Brady's or the Patriots' official Facebook pages, and nearly half didn't follow any NFL team.[14] It was a particularly effective complement to his TB12-themed book.[15] Brady is a masterful communicator with his team, and it's clear his abilities go beyond the locker room as well. His ability to create authentic, interesting content helped his brand and company grow.

LEADERSHIP LESSONS FROM THE FIELD:

- Leaders must communicate effectively in whatever way their team needs. They understand that even the most compelling messaging won't be meaningful if it never reaches its intended audience. The best leaders use the type of communication, method of distribution, content, and tone best suited to their team.
- Storytelling is a great way to deliver important information. Effective leaders can translate key themes, strong examples, and motivation into stories that make an emotional connection with team members.
- Communication as a leader is most effective when treated as a regular practice, as opposed to an occasional whim. Build the audience, keep them engaged, and then deliver useful information. They will follow and keep coming back for more.

MAKE YOURSELF HEARD

It's hard to coalesce a group around a shared vision and get them all moving in the same direction. It takes compelling communication, in a tone the audience appreciates, delivered in an accessible way. And it has to be genuine, because people can spot inauthenticity from a mile away. Seventy-two percent of employees don't have a firm grasp of their company's strategy,[16] and disengaged employees cost companies $450 billion annually.[17] In a world with millions of competing stimuli at home and at work, it's no easy task to craft a message that not only stands out, but also stays.

Leaders command attention from those around them. They get in the heads of their teammates, and their message sticks. They use a variety of methods to make sure each person on the team gets it. Leaders are honest and vulnerable and are always armed with stories and examples of ideal behavior. If you are near perfect, few will relate to you. Great leaders expose their humanity so they are approachable. Brady shows his emotions, from losing his cool on the sidelines to crying on camera about painful memories, but he uses all of it to motivate himself and his teammates. At its core, decision-making is an emotional process.[18] People remember messages that make an emotional connection with them. Emotion comes from humor, trauma, or beauty. Whatever the information and delivery method, leaders need to generate at least one of these emotions in order to make their messages break through the noise and then stand the test of time.

Most people love to laugh. With humor, you can quickly create a shared experience and establish rapport. And since many people like to share funny things, hilarity has a long tail. Think about a funny Super Bowl ad you still remember months later, or a silly jingle you can't get out of your head. Humor is effective! Even Brady is known to get into locker room pranks,[19] which makes him human and endears him to his team. There are many types of humor, including slapstick, situational, ironic, sarcastic, etc., but leaders need to choose their comedy carefully. You and your organization can't afford to be perceived as offensive or unserious. It's OK to have your audience laugh at you, but in every other scenario, your audience should feel you are laughing *with* them, not *at* them.

You can also capture someone's attention through a shocking, distressing, or disturbing experience. The feelings may not be pleasant, but they are powerful, memorable, and create urgency. You know the ads with hungry babies or abused animals. They're distressing and cringeworthy, but they stick! When Brady yells angrily on the sidelines, he's trying to inspire emotion in his teammates. Messaging with trauma may tug the heartstrings and evoke sadness by presenting a tragedy. It may induce disgust by depicting an outrage, moral failing, or physically repellent situation. It may shock and frighten the audience by illustrating a danger to themselves or others. Like humor, trauma requires a careful hand. You want to rouse people, but need to avoid truly hurting them or making them feel manipulated.

Beauty evokes what is best, most enjoyable, and moving to people. Poetic language, striking color and form, and graceful movement can stimulate a pleasing sense of calm or peace. You may have seen commercials for a tropical destination with romancing couples, families on jet skis, and solitary figures basking in the sun. The scenes they depict evoke a sense of longing in the audience. Brady posts videos of himself working out with TB12 equipment and tries to make the audience feel his method is totally accessible. Just remember that one person's beauty may be another person's trauma, so make sure you know your audience.

No matter what kind of emotional connection a leader seeks, it won't mean anything if the audience can't hear it. That's why the best leaders learn to use a variety of multimedia tools to express their messages efficiently and effectively. Leaders understand how best to reach their team and are willing and able to use whatever channel necessary. Baby boomers, for example, probably aren't going to check a Snapchat account, but it may be a great way to reach Gen Zers. It's true that Tom Brady can hire professional production teams to create his videos and craft his messages. Effective leaders can still do a lot on a more modest budget. There are so many ways to share information, from live presentations, to text in a newsletter, to images on a poster, to slide decks, and more. They don't have to be flashy; they just have to be compelling.

As Brady learned, one great way to share compelling messaging with an emotional connection is through storytelling. In fact, people are more than 20 times more likely to retain information they receive as part of a story.[20] Meaningful storytelling is an excellent way to embed crucial information in a memorable way. The best leaders don't talk about themselves too much, so they search for stories from inside their own team. It's a way to point out a good performance, while also explaining what other team members should be doing. Stories can get conveyed in a lot of different multimedia formats.

ACTION FROM THE BUSINESS STADIUM: COMMUNICATING ACROSS LANGUAGES

Torrie was the CEO of a home health aid company looking to improve customer ratings and grow. Like Brady, Torrie decided to take a holistic approach, using the opportunity to revamp the company's core values and improve internal communications to make customers happier with the service they received. Over the course of several months, Torrie and her executive team researched, discussed, refined, and finally selected updated core values and a clear mission statement.

The team also designed an excellent rollout process that used improved internal communications to spread the word about the new core values. Many employees were not native speakers of English, so they made sure all the internal communications were available in the languages necessary. Just as Brady uses compelling messaging and multiple social media tools, they emailed regular newsletters and posted signs in the corporate office and the company's group homes. They even introduced a brief weekly podcast featuring the CEO and other executives in which they shared best practices, industry insights, and company updates. They also instituted a rewards program where strong performers received extra time off. Torrie and the executive team were excited to see how the new program would improve employee practices and eventually increase customer ratings.

Unfortunately, after a few months, nothing changed. Torrie gathered her executive team to problem solve.

"It's not working, and I'm not sure why. Our employee metrics are totally stagnant, and there's no change in customer feedback," lamented Torrie.

"Our data shows that employees are generally reading the newsletters and listening to the podcasts. The signs are all posted prominently in high-traffic locations," stated Gregory, vice president of human resources. "Employees are getting exposed to the material, but for whatever reason, they're not absorbing it."

"Anyone have thoughts?" asked Torrie.

"We've tried to take language barrier into account," commented Noelle, another executive. "But I wonder if we still haven't quite solved the problem. Our newsletters and signs are in multiple languages, but are we sure they're fully comprehending what's there? Can they follow the content of the podcast well enough to put it to good use?"

"That's an interesting point, Noelle," said Torrie. "Gregory, what does the data say about employee retention of our new core values?"

"They're not great," he responded. "We sent a cute little game with the last newsletter, where employees could match related words to the core value it represented. We thought it would be a good way to make the core values clear to non-native English speakers, using synonyms they might be more familiar with. About half the employees played it, and their scores were low."

"Well they would be, wouldn't they?" commented Noelle. "It's a nice idea to confront the language difference that way, and it might have helped a few people, but using a thesaurus doesn't really solve the problem."

"OK, so we need a better way to explain what these core values mean, what they look like. Any ideas?" Torrie asked.

"What about telling a story, relating it to something employees already know?" proposed Gregory. He continued, "We could ask middle managers for examples of employees taking some action that illustrates the core value. Not all employees will understand every word, but they'll understand the arc of what's happening between the patient and health care aide."

"I like that idea," said Torrie. "We could add it as a segment of the podcast, maybe feature that individual in the newsletter. A quick story of one of their own colleagues doing something that demonstrates a core value. Comprehensible and relatable."

Torrie and the team went right to work finding examples and figuring out how to share them in a brief, compelling story. One week Torrie explained the concept of advocating for the patient with the story of a home health aide who mentioned a recurring ailment during the patient's doctor's appointment, which uncovered a larger but treatable problem that improved the patient's quality of life. Another week Torrie explained going the extra mile with the story of an aide who installed some padding on a piece of furniture she noticed the patient would often bump his hip.

After a few months, the executives noticed a huge difference in the data. Just as Brady used storytelling and multimedia to grow his following and build his brand, Torrie had used it to improve employee performance and increase customer ratings. Consumption of the newsletter and podcast became almost universal. Managers were delighted to bring attention to their star performers. A few employees made suggestions for new posters and signs. More aides could actually recite the core values and explain what they meant. Customers were clearly happy based on their survey feedback, and the company's referrals went way up. The company grew, and Torrie continued to use multimedia in effective ways to engage employees and create better patient outcomes.

GAME REVIEW:

- Simply sharing information is an ineffective way of communicating. Leaders need to do more than just state facts. They must package it in a way that is interesting to the audience and will make the message stick.
- The best leaders are comfortable using a variety of different methods and formats of communication. They reach out to their team members where they are and present content that's easy to absorb.
- Storytelling is a powerful tool to illustrate behavior and encourage compliance. It increases audience comprehension and can inspire similar action.

EXECUTING THE PLAY

Exercises for the Preseason:

- Evaluate your team's core values. Does each member of your team know what they are and understand what they mean? How can you remind your team of their importance and encourage best practices?
- Make a list of stories, from both within and outside your team, that illustrate a behavior you want your team to notice. Remember that the behavior could be good or bad. How could you work some of these stories into your team communication?
- Create a media plan, including type and frequency, that reaches your team where they live—most likely on their phones. Gain some basic proficiency in using your own phone to produce compelling content, and put it out to the team regularly.

Best Practices for the Game:

- When you see a team member do something great, share it with the rest of the team. Highly relatable, real-world examples are both descriptive and inspiring.
- Experiment with a variety of multimedia formats to present information to your team. Ask them which communication modes they like the best, and try to create content that really speaks to them. You'll learn a ton by doing!
- Ask your team for ideas about content and stories to be used in your internal communications. Team members often have stellar examples that leaders don't know about. Even better, ask your team to create content using multimedia.

PART IV
Seizing the Trophies

CHAPTER 10

Executing Team Success

"We've been rewarded with something that the scoreboard won't show—the satisfaction of knowing we gave everything to each other in pursuit of a common goal. That is what TEAM is all about."[1]
—Tom Brady, to his team via Instagram

PRACTICE WINS CHAMPIONSHIPS

Malcolm Butler couldn't believe it. Just a few years before, he was kicked off his community college team and had to get a job at a fast food restaurant.[2] Then he played at the University of West Alabama, a Division II school.[3] He performed terribly at his pro day and didn't get drafted.[4] He had to beg the New England Patriots to invite him to their rookie minicamp.[5] Yet there he was, a rookie in the NFL, in uniform for Super Bowl XLIX. He was on the same team as Tom Brady and Rob Gronkowski. They were playing the Seattle Seahawks, a team comprised of talented quarterback Russell Wilson, the notorious "Legion of Boom" defense, and a 215-pound, five-time Pro Bowler machine of a running back Marshawn "Beast Mode" Lynch.[6] It felt unreal, like a dream too good to come true.

Butler wasn't sure whether he'd play. He knew he had a good week of practice,[7] but it's hard to predict how coaches determine playing time in the playoffs. In the first half of the game, Butler didn't see the field.[8] In the third quarter, though, things started to change. The Seahawks opened a 10-point lead,[9] and the Patriots' defensive coordinator benched the player ahead of Butler.[10]

All season, Butler modeled his work ethic on what he saw in Tom Brady. They played on different sides of the ball, but the model was the same: be consistent and take care of your business so you can prepare thoroughly and be ready for unexpected changes. And Butler *was* ready. He recorded his first tackle of the game against Lynch, who outweighed him considerably. Butler continued to play well, making tackles and breaking up passes through the fourth quarter.[11] With Butler and the defense playing better, Brady and the offense chipped away at the Seahawks' lead.[12]

Just before the two-minute warning, the Patriots scored a touchdown and an extra point for a four-point lead.[13] The challenge for the Seahawks was time—there was too much of it. Two minutes was more than enough time for the Seahawks to drive down the field and reclaim the lead with a touchdown. The bigger problem was designing the drive so the Seahawks scored as late as possible, thereby leaving the Patriots no time for a last-second drive of their own.

After a few downs, Wilson threw a deep pass down the right sideline to Seahawks wide receiver Jermaine Kearse.[14] Butler was right on Kearse from the line of scrimmage, playing tight coverage and putting himself in good position. It was textbook technique, like Brady drilled for every week. At just the right moment, Butler turned his head, saw the pass coming, and twisted his body to make a play on the ball.[15] He jumped and reached up and managed to get his hand between Kearse's. The ball deflected off their hands, and both players fell to the ground.[16] *I stopped it!* Butler must have thought. But Butler noticed Kearse was still moving on the ground. Somehow, Kearse caught the ball! Butler was up in a flash, and tackled Kearse out of bounds to narrowly avoid a Seahawks touchdown.

Kearse's catch was the stuff of movies. To most people in the stadium and watching on TV, it looked like a great defensive play that led to an incomplete pass. By incredible luck, when Kearse fell, the tipped ball bounced off his legs instead of falling to the ground. With the unpredictable physics of an oblong ball careening off a round leg, the ball bounced in the direction of Kearse's arms, and the momentum from Kearse's fall kept his body moving in the same direction as the bounce. Kearse juggled the ball for a few moments, but ultimately managed to secure it.[17]

Butler was gutted.[18] He did everything right: he stuck to his man, played tight but clean, made a great play on the ball, and managed to knock the pass off trajectory. He even had the presence of mind to notice the play was still alive after he fell. And still, all Butler's effort was for naught: Kearse caught the ball, and the Seahawks were five yards from what was likely a game-winning touchdown. Butler went to the sideline and angrily pulled at the chin strap on his helmet.[19]

Despite his apparent disappointment, Butler knew he had only a moment to recover and move on. Brady taught him that football players need to have short memories. After all, Brady threw two interceptions earlier in the game, one of which led to a Seahawks touchdown.[20] Still, Brady continued leading the team, inspiring his guys, and pushing the ball down the field. To keep modeling Brady, Butler knew he had to move past Kearse's great play and prepare himself for the next down. The game wasn't over. The Seahawks were close, but they still had to actually put the ball in the end zone. Butler and his Patriots were known for their bend-but-not-break defense. Plus they had Brady, master of short memories and fourth quarter game-winning drives.

A running play got the Seahawks to the Patriots' 1-yard line.[21] As Wilson and the Seahawks broke their huddle, Butler ran back onto the field, ready to dig in.[22] Conventional wisdom said this had to be another running play. It was a short yardage situation. Seattle was trying to run down the clock to leave New England no time, and an incomplete pass would stop the clock. Most of all, the Seahawks had Marshawn Lynch, their surefire running back.

So Butler was surprised when he examined the Seahawks' alignment. *Three receivers on a goal line play? There are usually only two on the goal line.* Something tingled in the back of Butler's mind. He thought back to the week of practice and the team's film preparation. *I saw this lineup with the scout team. It's a pass play. I got beat for a touchdown on this look.*[23] Belichick was not happy when it happened. "If you see that formation, you have to just jump it," he demanded of Butler. Brady always learned from his mistakes, and Butler would too. *I won't get beat twice.*

The Seahawks snapped the ball. Butler didn't move and instead watched his assigned receiver. The moment his receiver cut inside, Butler broke full speed to the spot the ball would be thrown. The players collided; Butler snagged the ball as his opponent repelled to the ground. Butler steadied himself and scrambled as far as he could out of the end zone.[24] The game was essentially over; the Patriots won the Super Bowl.

It was a remarkable play. Just as remarkable as the play, however, was the preparation that went into it. Brady comes so prepared to every practice and every game that his teammates must do the same in order to keep up with him. Belichick expected the same high standards. Further, Belichick spotted in Butler the same untapped potential he saw in Brady. So just as Brady had, Butler worked with Belichick and the defensive coaches all season to realize it.[25]

In preparing for the Super Bowl, Brady and the Patriots studied the Seahawks carefully. They examined specific scenarios and how Seattle tended to respond. They looked at all of Seattle's offensive plays that year from the goal line.[26]

Then the team practiced those scenarios. By drilling this information into the players and repeatedly practicing for specific situations, Brady and Belichick wanted to improve their muscle memory. It's difficult to practice for high-pressure scenarios because it's nearly impossible to recreate the game atmosphere and emotion. Brady and Belichick, however, knew that great preparation could help minimize the emotion, allowing players to lean on their instincts. And when

Butler lined up and saw stacked receivers, that's exactly what happened.

Just as he saw Brady do so many times before, Butler pushed aside his emotions, including the frustration of his prior play and the stress of the moment. He followed the same procedure he used in every snap of every practice and game to analyze the offensive lineup. He recalled the specific prior result when he gave up a touchdown and did exactly as he was instructed to jump the route.

Brady was delighted by Butler's big play. He understood exactly how hard Butler worked all season. Brady also knew the play—and ultimately the outcome of the Super Bowl—wasn't the result of luck. Butler's performance was the direct result of the repeated, specific preparation and practice that Brady inspired and the coaches enacted. Brady was so impressed by the moment—the culmination of Butler's season of relentless work—that Brady gave Butler the pickup truck he received for being named Super Bowl MVP.[27] Later, Brady said of the play, "It all leads to that particular moment. You put a lot of hard work in over the course of the season and Malcolm did that. To recognize a formation, a play, put it all together in your mind as a young player, it was the perfect play at the perfect time."[28]

LEADERSHIP LESSONS FROM THE FIELD:

- The best leaders leave no stone unturned. They examine every angle, consider every possibility, and game plan solutions for each. Then they make sure each member of the team understands all the wrinkles.
- Teams need practice. Effective leaders understand that simply sharing information isn't enough—they need to guide their team through repetitive, effective practice.

In one play, Malcolm Butler ripped out the hearts of Seattle fans. While Butler rightly received many accolades for his heady, timely play, it took more than just his individual effort to make it come together. As Brady knew, the interception was not random chance—it was a calculated effort. The moment highlighted Brady's masterful preparatory approach and how he inspires the same in his teammates.

Brady and the Patriots practiced the same way every week, from Week 1 through the playoffs.[29] Practices were intense and incredibly detail-oriented. The Patriots' physical conditioning trained them for specific game scenarios. For example, the players practiced a punt at full speed and pretend a penalty was called. To mimic the play clock, they walked back up the field and immediately executed another punt.[30] All of this was to recreate the experience of game day and prepare the players for peak performance through the fourth quarter.[31]

Patriots' practice was always the same, and it was brutal, but it worked. When other teams got tired in the fourth quarter, the Patriots were still energized. Exhausted opponents move slower and get sloppy with technique; the Patriots suffered from neither problem. Brady's dropback footwork and throwing mechanics are identical, whether it's the first down of the game or overtime. Brady and his teammates probably get tired and frustrated and maybe even a little angry as they run drill after drill, do sprint after sprint. But Brady leads by example, demonstrating a willingness to undergo such tough practices and the mental fortitude to push his emotions aside and execute the plan. Brady is human, after all, and may not love the physical pain or mental endurance—but he loves that it helps the team win on Sundays, and he makes sure his teammates understand the connection.

Brady and Belichick would also run a great deal of situational training during practice. Every week, the Patriots prepared just like they prepared for the Seahawks' goal-line offense with three receivers. Butler said of the Seahawks' alignment, "I knew they were stacked . . . It all comes from preparation. I knew they were doing a pick right or coming under . . . I just went and made a play."[32] Surely other Patriots could have made similar claims of prescience throughout the season. The Patriots' situational training helped the team know exactly what is coming in any scenario. Repetition is particularly necessary: after only 48 hours, people forget as much as 60 percent of what they learned.[33]

Brady understands that all teams need consistent, specific, reinforced training regimens that prepare them for real-world scenarios. In sports and business, leaders need to make sure their teams can execute the systems and follow the processes the leaders put in place. Without practice and constructive feedback, leaders can't expect their teams to perform well. When a crisis arises, a team shouldn't be executing the response plan for the first time.

The reality is that things fall apart and failure happens. Effective leaders don't just train for success—they train for problems, too. Even if a team has a playbook of what to do in a crisis, it probably won't do much good if they haven't practiced the play. Teams need to practice applying specific skills and managing their emotions. That's why Brady encourages practice players to intercept him (see Chapter 5), even though it makes him furious. Failure is an opportunity to learn and improve. Brady understands that the old adage is true—practice makes perfect (or at least gets you a lot closer to perfection).

Leaders also need to ensure they're taking advantage of the skills of every member of their team. It's important for leaders to make the most of the talent available. It helps make the whole team feel involved and encourages every member to take ownership of the project. Throughout the season, Belichick invested time in Butler because he saw Butler's potential and understood individuals need to be challenged and engaged. Brady, too, encouraged Butler every week in practice and ultimately rewarded the proof of his intense preparation with a pickup truck. Teams with high levels of engagement achieve more than 20 percent higher productivity and profitability.[34] In the search for opportunities to help teammates grow, you can also uncover hidden talents you didn't know they had and can help your team become more efficient.

ACTION FROM THE BUSINESS STADIUM: USING PAPERWORK TO MAKE PAPER

Business coach Dan Larson shared the story of a wealth management company that hired him in the 1990s to develop their playbook and redirect their sales strategy. The company was quite successful, with considerable assets under management, a strong culture, and a proud history. The CEO, Eric, was so pleased with Dan's work that the company brought Dan back several times to update their playbooks, refine strategies, and identify opportunities.

During one visit, Dan and Eric walked out of the conference room on their way to an off-site meeting. As they passed the front desk, Eric spoke with the receptionist, Lauren, who assisted in a number of administrative duties.

"Hey, Lauren, anything back yet from the Bakers?" Eric asked.

"Sorry, nothing yet. I'll let you know if anything comes in," she replied, looking a bit disappointed.

Eric's face fell in response, so at lunch later that day, Dan asked Eric about it.

"A couple weeks ago, we made a presentation to the Bakers. They're a young married couple who've been very successful so far. They're super friendly and smart, and they're looking to set up a successful retirement plan. They loved the plan we proposed, appreciated that it prioritized saving and investing but still left enough flexibility for a decent lifestyle now. It was basically a done deal—they gave a verbal commitment and said they'd sign the documents right away. But when we sent them the paperwork, they never sent it back," Eric said.

"That's frustrating," Dan replied. "But things fall through in sales all the time. Is there something different about the Bakers?"

"No, it's not them specifically," Eric said. "It's just too bad when deals look done, but don't close. Each member of the team executes the sales playbook perfectly. We identify potential clients through the lead generation process, we send them our polished marketing collateral, and we use our scripts when we talk to them. We present a strong financial plan and really click with a potential client . . . and then they don't sign on the dotted line."

"You guys have a pretty good conversion rate though. How often does this happen? Is this something we need to address in your playbook?" asked Dan.

"No, no," dismissed Eric. "I'm just venting. Everyone in the company gets down about it. But that's just how it is in this business. I have colleagues in other wealth management firms and they complain of the same exact problem. Paperwork just gets in the way. But ultimately you have to have signatures on the page. There's no way around it."

Dan reflected on what Eric said. In any industry, there are inefficiencies that can't be totally resolved. Even Tom Brady doesn't throw a perfect pass every time on every receiver route. But just because a problem can't be completely *fixed* doesn't mean it can't be *improved*. That's why Brady and his receivers practice and communicate so much: so they can increase the odds of success. Brady is also able to push aside his emotions to clear his mind and ensure consistent performance, but it seemed like Eric and his team were often frustrated by the state of affairs.

"Eric, it sounds like you think this isn't a big deal. And maybe it is minor, but it's clearly bothering you all. I'd like to explore it with you. In my experience, many people assume the status quo is unchangeable, that it's just a fact of life. But really, there's often more room for movement than they think," shared Dan.

Eric agreed, and when they got back to the office, he explained to Dan how the signing process worked.

"After the account executive delivers the detailed presentation and proposal to the potential clients, they have to decide what they want to do," Eric explained. "Our playbook is pretty effective, and most of the time, they're ready to become our clients."

"And they don't just sign in the office?" asked Dan.

"The paperwork's too long and complicated to do in the office," Eric said. "There are a bunch of forms to fill out, and clients need to get paperwork from their current banking institutions to move the money over to us. Plus some clients want to get the contract reviewed by attorneys, and some live out of state so they're not in the office to begin with."

"So what happens with the paperwork?" Dan asked.

"So the account executive gets all the paperwork together and does as much of the leg work for the clients as they can. It usually takes a couple days, sometimes a little longer. Then they give it to Lauren to overnight it to the clients," Eric stated. (Remember, this was the 1990s, so electronic documents and digital signatures weren't an option.)

"And of these potential clients who are ready to sign on the dotted line after the presentation—how many of them ultimately sign the paperwork and send it back to you?" posed Dan.

"Maybe about 25 percent. Poor Lauren's always the one reporting the bad news," said Eric. When Dan's eyes widened, Eric continued, "That's not bad, actually. I have some competitors that get more like 10 or 15 percent."

Dan was incredulous.

"Twenty-five percent? These people are enthusiastic about becoming your clients, have verbally agreed—and a full *three quarters* of them don't return the paperwork? And that's *good*?" Dan asked.

"I told you," said Eric as he shook his head. "It's just a reality of wealth management."

Dan was shocked. He couldn't believe this was an immutable truth of the industry. When Brady identifies a problem, he doesn't take it for granted as unsolvable. He explores options and comes up with creative ideas. And even if he discovers it can't be solved, he at least uncovers ways to mitigate it. Moreover, Brady demonstrates how to overcome his emotions and focus on execution. There's no time for down spirits. Dan wanted to do the same for Eric and his company. Surely this conversion rate didn't have to remain so low, or afflict the team with such negative feelings. Dan continued thinking about and trouble-shooting it long after his visit. By the time Dan was ready for his next visit to the company, he had developed a plan.

"Here's the problem," started Dan. "Your account executives are just sending out these packets of documents. But no one is reminding the potential clients that they're coming, right?"

Eric nodded.

"But people are busy. Young couples come to you because they need to start saving for college for the kid they just had—which means they're distracted and could forget about paperwork. Older people come to you as they're preparing for retirement and planning a future full of grandkids and vacations—so they're distracted too. Maybe a client is on a business trip when the paperwork arrives, and it gets neglected in the pile of mail they return to. A thousand things can happen to get in the way!" exclaimed Dan.

"So what do you propose?" asked Eric.

"It's actually pretty simple," said Dan. "When Lauren gets paperwork from an account executive, don't have her send the packet out right away. Instead, have her call the potential client to confirm they'll be ready to receive it. She can also gently suggest a timeframe for returning the paperwork.

"It's a win all around. Reminding clients about the paperwork is good customer service. They'll appreciate your consideration of their time and your willingness to delay the paperwork if they're not home to receive it. Plus it's an opening for them to ask last-minute questions they might want clarified. And you've told me Lauren is very capable and great with the clients. This is an opportunity for her to interact with them more often and to play a critical role in the sales process. Plus she won't have to deliver bad news of no paperwork so often. This will make your company more efficient and engage more of your team," concluded Dan.

"That's . . . a terrific idea," said Eric. "I can't believe no one thought of it before."

"Actually, it makes a lot of sense," Dan commented. "You said the whole industry has always had this problem. So everyone thought it wasn't actually a *problem*—just a reality everyone had to deal with. Now, you can develop an effective process for your team to counteract it. I think it could really contribute to your positive culture."

Eric and Dan shared their plan with the account executives and Lauren, and they all agreed to the plan. Lauren in particular was excited to be given an important new responsibility. Like Malcolm Butler, Lauren was new to the team, but eager to learn and very coachable. Eric and Dan trained the account executives on the new process, and they gave Lauren a playbook with a script that contained answers to likely questions.

A month later, Eric and Dan reviewed the results, and they were not disappointed. Previously, just 25 percent of clients who received paperwork actually returned it. In only 30 days, with those minor adjustments in process, the rate increased to 80 percent. Eric and his company spent the same amount of money on staffing, marketing, and shipping, but with the increased conversion rate, they suddenly got paid four times more than they had been. From then on, Eric tried never to assume that a problem was unfixable, and his relationship with Dan remained strong and productive.

GAME REVIEW:

- Great leaders don't make assumptions about what can and can't be done. They watch for hidden problems and develop processes to solve or counteract them. Then they train their team and regularly practice the proper response.
- The best leaders look for ways to involve every member of the team in critical processes. It helps build camaraderie, develop team members' skills, and identify opportunities for increased efficiency.

EXECUTING THE PLAY

Exercises for the Preseason:

- Think about the processes in place for various functions within your own team. Are there shortcomings you assume are unavoidable? Are there other elements that seem inefficient or outdated? Approach each process with fresh eyes, and see if there are opportunities to improve how your team operates.

- Is there a member of your team who frequently seems to draw the short straw? Is anyone underappreciated or not given many opportunities to demonstrate their potential? How can you capitalize on that person's skills and involve them in a critical team function? Or perhaps *you're* that team member. Can you demonstrate leadership and advocate for yourself by suggesting a process improvement to which you can contribute?

Best Practices for the Game:

- The next time a teammate gets frustrated that their performance isn't making a difference, remind them that their next opportunity for greatness is just around the corner. Malcolm Butler made a great defensive play on the pass to Jermaine Kearse, but Kearse still caught the ball. Just a few plays later, Butler got another chance and changed the course of the Super Bowl. He couldn't have done it if he hadn't modeled Brady's ability to overcome emotions.

- As a team, review the problem-solving processes in place. Make sure they're up to date, thorough, and clearly identify everyone's roles. Then practice! Evaluate what goes well and what needs improvement. Then practice again!

CHAPTER 11

Attitude Is Everything

"I'm only as good as the guys around me and they're only as good as I am. Part of that is motivating each other so that we can all be on the same page and all be at our best."[1]
—Tom Brady

TEAM LEADERS ARE TEAM MEMBERS, TOO

Chad Johnson was a star. The extremely talented Cincinnati Bengals wide receiver was a six-time Pro Bowler and two-time First Team All Pro.[2] Johnson was also not afraid to be the center of attention: he was among the most influential athletes on social media[3] and one of the biggest showboats in professional sports.[4] In fact, at the time, his legal last name was Ochocinco, which he changed to reflect his jersey number 85.[5]

Many megastars in professional sports expect to be treated a certain way. They usually don't like to be criticized in front of their teammates and often have enough influence to silence their coaches. Plus, some accused Johnson's coach in Cincinnati, Marvin Lewis, of failing to enforce discipline on the team.[6] So Johnson may have felt that he and other stars were entitled to that kind of treatment and could expect it in every locker room.

After being traded from Cincinnati to New England in the 2011 offseason,[7] Johnson must have been curious to see how he would be treated there. As a wide receiver, he likely was excited to work with arguably the best quarterback in the league, Tom Brady. But Johnson's enthusiasm was probably tempered by what he'd no doubt heard about coach Bill Belichick: gruff, exacting, sarcastic, and worse. Johnson might have worried his own big personality could clash with Belichick's. He may have been concerned he would have difficulty adjusting to the famous "Patriot Way."[8]

When he arrived in Foxborough on the first day, Johnson wasn't surprised the day began with a team meeting.[9] Perhaps he anticipated a warm welcome or a pep talk of some sort, as it had been with Lewis and the Bengals. Johnson knew Belichick could be harsh, but surely even Belichick wanted to start the season off on a positive note. Johnson entered the meeting room and selected a seat. Soon, Belichick walked into the room. Without so much as a greeting, Belichick queued the tape of the Patriots' last game—a disappointing loss to the rival New York Jets in the AFC divisional round of the playoffs that January.[10]

With barely contained rage, Belichick lit into the team, pointing out every single thing they did wrong. There were big things, like running the wrong route or missing an assignment. And then there was minutiae. Belichick zoomed in on one lineman's hands, furious at the sloppy technique.[11] He criticized another lineman's first step—and then replayed it four times, finding new flaws with each viewing.[12]

Then Belichick turned his attention to Tom Brady, one of the greatest quarterbacks of all time, already a three-time Super Bowl champion and perennial Pro Bowler. Belichick used a calm, if menacing, voice to describe other players' mistakes on the tape, and Johnson probably expected Belichick to tone it down when it came to Brady. Instead, Belichick unleashed. He actually yelled, even got up in Brady's face while he did it.[13] Belichick highlighted every single mistake Brady made. As a final insult, he berated Brady with, "The quarterback at Foxborough High could make that throw."[14]

Johnson was stunned. *Is this a joke? Are we being punked?*[15] How could Belichick chastise Brady so ruthlessly, so publicly? Johnson couldn't even imagine his reaction if a coach spoke to him that way, especially in front of others. Johnson had never seen anything like it in his career. Brady could have sat dejected, argued with Belichick, defended himself, or even stormed out. It's not as if Brady hadn't proven himself time and time again. He had earned the right to a pass in a team film session. Surely Brady wouldn't stand for it.

And yet when Johnson looked, he saw Brady hyper-focused on Belichick. There was no trace of anger on Brady's face, just concentration as he took detailed notes. When Belichick's tirade was finally over and Brady finished writing, he looked up at Belichick and nodded.

What?! Johnson couldn't believe it. Brady never even flinched as Belichick went at him. It almost seemed as if Brady liked it. He scribbled notes as Belichick mentioned even the most mundane details. Later on in practice, if Brady saw a mistake Belichick mentioned during the film session, Brady pointed it out. If Brady repeated a mistake he made on film, he would get visibly angry with himself. Brady constantly reinforced Belichick's messages in his own behavior and in his explanations to teammates during organized and ad hoc meetings.

To Johnson, it seemed that whatever Belichick said, Brady used as fire. His ego was nowhere to be found as Belichick practically belittled him. He stored it up to fuel his competitive spirit and to light the same spark in his teammates. Whatever criticism was thrown his way, Brady used as a learning tool and motivational message. Nothing could get Brady down; no adversity was too big to overcome. Johnson watched in awe all season as Brady withstood Belichick's tirades, calmly brought his team through every challenge, and eventually led the Patriots to yet another Super Bowl appearance. His attitude and spirit were indomitable.

LEADERSHIP LESSONS FROM THE FIELD:

- Great leaders thrive in moments of adversity. They are prepared for anything that comes their way. Win or lose, there is always knowledge to gain from the experience. Leaders exemplify in their own behavior that the team's attitude towards defeat will determine future outcomes.
- Leaders are prepared to take their lumps. Even though they're in charge, they're not above anyone else on the team. They hold themselves to the same standards and face the same consequences for their actions. Great leaders are fair, transparent, and authentic.
- The most effective leaders build the team's confidence. They do this by reinforcing key messaging, explaining why their plan is smart, and practicing team execution. They generate a positive attitude throughout the team.

GROWING THROUGH PAIN

Brady isn't just the *leader* of his team—he's also a *member* of the team. He goes through every step of preseason preparations, daily practices and film sessions, game day fights, and physical treatments that the team does. Brady is one with his team, even though he surely could get away with distancing himself. He allowed Belichick to treat him coarsely so he never lost the drive to improve. It kept him humble, demonstrated to his teammates the proper approach, and helped him keep track of what was most important. He'll surely allow Bucs coaches to treat him as if he were any other player as well.

One of Brady's most important leadership qualities is his ability to lead his team through difficult times. Part of his effectiveness is in his ability to view the fight through the same perspective as his teammates. In every football game, during every season, throughout every career, there are inevitably struggles.

They may feel insurmountable, and indeed, sometimes they may be. What makes great leaders—whether they are designated as a leader or not—is their ability to push their team through to the other side. If there's a problem, leaders fix it or find a way around it. If a team member lacks faith, leaders motivate him to continue. Through the fight, the team grows closer and becomes more efficient.

With Brady at the helm, the Patriots were able to overcome challenges because they were accustomed to it. All season long, Belichick created challenges for his team in ways large and small. He pushed them to their limits in practice and criticized their every move in film sessions. By creating a stressful environment in practice, Belichick made sure his team knew how to react to the stressful environment of a game. They knew the attitude they needed to embody in order to survive, and they knew whom to look towards for cues.

This is where Brady quietly but powerfully shines. As Chad Johnson witnessed, Brady didn't say a word as Belichick eviscerated him—yet Brady's reaction spoke volumes. When Brady accepted—even embraced—Belichick's harsh treatment and learned from it, everyone else understood they had to do the same. From the very first practice, the team learned to look towards Brady in moments of despair. He demonstrated how they should react to stressful situations. When it came time for the game, they were already used to following their leader and mirroring his attitude.

As Jim Collins points out when he explains the Stockdale Paradox;[16] simple optimism isn't the attitude that will get you through challenges; instead, you need unshakable faith that you will survive, combined with the discipline to accept the reality of your situation. Brady has withstood adversity throughout his career, so his teammates know they can trust him the next time a challenge arises. From struggling in the beginning of his high school and college days, to being drafted in the sixth round, to being the last on the depth chart in New England, Brady has overcome it all with a strong belief in himself and dedication to his plan.

Brady takes the same approach to motivating his team. When he led his team back from 25 points down in Super Bowl LI (see Chapter 3), Brady didn't cajole his team with a "rah-rah" message. Instead, he reminded his teammates that the game wasn't over and then skillfully executed their plan one play at a time. His calm demeanor throughout it all demonstrated his belief in his team. No panic was necessary—they were prepared to handle the challenge.

The same perspective is required in business: success demands a positive attitude coupled with a pragmatic approach. Just like Brady understands, members of the team need to believe in the quality of their game plan and have confidence in their ability to execute it at a high level. If they expect their team to perform in the face of adversity, leaders must demonstrate their own belief in these elements. They can motivate their teams by explaining they are capable of great success due to their hard work and superior plan and then calmly lead them down the path. Brady's approach is infectious.

ACTION FROM THE BUSINESS STADIUM: GAINING THE MENTAL EDGE

Business coach Dan Larson shared his experience working with a Canadian boat crane manufacturer whose salespeople didn't realize the remarkable quality of the product they were selling. The founder and CEO, Craig, was a lifelong boating enthusiast who had been in the marine industry his whole career. Craig was also highly intelligent and believed most modern boat cranes left a great deal to be desired. When he founded the company seven years prior, his goal was to create a better, lighter, more efficient crane that would provide superior service to consumers and better protect the value of their boats. To that end, Craig hired an aeronautical engineer, Jake, to help him design the cranes.

Craig built the company into a small but successful business, but after a few years, it hit a wall. Despite having high-quality products and a satisfied customer base, Craig found it difficult to expand his market share. It would be as if Brady's teams became a good team, but never transformed into great ones. There were a few big competitors that dominated the market, and Craig just couldn't seem to get his sales team to break the stranglehold. He decided to ask Dan for help. Dan set up a meeting with Craig and Jake to better understand the product and the company's processes.

"So Craig, tell me more about your company and what's going on," began Dan.

"I'm not sure why we're having so much difficulty," admitted Craig. "We make good cranes, and Jake can prove it. We have a talented enough sales team, and they're all boaters, so they can speak the language. I designed a playbook that gives them sales scripts, answers to common questions and challenges, and decent marketing materials. We just can't crack our competition."

Dan noticed that Jake seemed eager to interject.

"Jake, what do I need to know about your cranes? In non-aeronautical terms, please!" said Dan.

"Yeah, look. I think Craig is seriously underselling our products. I don't normally like to toot my own horn, but toot toot!" Dan laughed as Jake continued, "Our cranes aren't good—they're great. They're made with super high-quality materials, have lower volume and weight, are more efficient, have better corrosion prevention, and more. We have thirty-eight different models, and every single one is as good or better than any competitor's equivalent model."

"Well that must certainly make the sales process much easier," commented Dan.

"You'd think so," responded Jake, "but it just doesn't translate to customers."

"Why do you think that is?" asked Dan.

"I think our sales people are frustrated. We've sort of hit a wall, and it's tough to make a sale. Our competitors can throw so many resources at their clients, offer discounts, have a bunch of slick marketing materials, all that kind of stuff," offered Craig.

"And it's hard to explain why our cranes are better. Our salespeople can speak boating lingo, but understandably, not many of them or our customers understand much about aeronautical design," added Jake.

To Dan, it seemed like the company had the framework of a smart sales process in place, but one that was neither robust nor exciting. Like Brady and his game plan, it appeared Craig and Jake had absolute faith in the product, but unlike Brady, they weren't convinced of their teammates' abilities to execute. Dan decided to discuss the situation with the sales people on the front lines in a candid group meeting.

"We're selling boat cranes. They're not exactly sexy," said one salesperson. "And our competitors are so huge. It feels impossible going up against Goliath every day."

"And at the end of the day, a crane is a crane, right? So all else being equal, potential customers are inclined to just stick with the manufacturer they already know," said another.

"But according to Jake, all else *isn't* equal. Apparently your boat cranes are way better," said Dan.

"I mean, he's an engineer, so I'm sure he's right," commented a third salesperson. "But it's hard to convince a customer that they're different enough to make a noticeable difference. Especially when our price point is a little higher and they're already satisfied with the product they've got."

Dan was surprised. The sales team was filled with boat people, yet even they seemed indifferent to their own products. Were the company's cranes really as great as Jake said they were? Was it enough to convince a potential customer to switch *and* spend more money? If the salespeople weren't convinced, how could the customers be? The sales team needed better guidance from the top. An NFL team is full of skilled players, and they may have a good game plan, but they still need Brady to coordinate them on their path to success. If Brady didn't believe in his teammates or the plan, how could he get others to follow him? Sales teams were no different.

To understand the customer perspective, Dan studied

the company's sales playbook and marketing materials. The product information and marketing materials laid out all the specs for each type of crane. The materials said how much the crane weighed, how large it was, how much it could lift, almost everything you'd want to know about it. But what did it all mean? Were the crane measurements any good? How did they compare to competitors' products? Dan wasn't surprised the salespeople weren't enthusiastic. Even Brady had to explain the functionality and beauty of Belichick's game plan to his teammates. How was anyone, even a boat person, supposed to make heads or tails of all these numbers?

"I want to do an experiment," Dan told Craig and Jake at their next meeting. "Pretend you're not a boat expert. You have a boat, you need a crane, but you're open to any brand.

"I've brought along some of your marketing materials. If you were that customer, what would you think about this product? Try to look at the information with fresh eyes."

Craig and Jake examined the material for a few moments.

"Well the numbers are really impressive, but I guess a regular customer wouldn't know that," admitted Craig.

"It would probably be hard for them to understand what they were looking at," agreed Jake.

"Now think about this," Dan continued. "Put yourself in the shoes of your salespeople. You're not an engineer, but you're a boat person, and you know a little something about cranes. What would you make of these materials?"

"I guess I might recognize that the numbers were good, although I probably wouldn't be so familiar with the numbers to be able to tell if they were *really* good, at least compared to what else is on the market," said Craig.

"If you were them, would you believe in the product you were selling?" asked Dan.

"Hmm. Maybe?" answered Craig, uncertain.

"So you think the problem is with our marketing materials we send to customers?" asked Jake.

"That's part of it, but it goes deeper than that," explained Dan. "You have this incredible product, but no one inside your company knows it. If salespeople don't understand why the cranes are so superior, how can they convince customers? If you were coaching a sports team, and you had designed a brilliant game plan you knew would totally confound the competition, wouldn't you tell your players, to give them a big confidence boost? You've never explained to your sales team how great these cranes are. They're sitting on a gold mine, but don't know it.

"The other thing is that I don't get the impression your sales team feels particularly motivated. They're not convinced you really believe in them. When leadership displays a defeatist attitude towards sales, the salespeople will start to feel the same way. You've told *me* they're capable—but you need to tell *them*, too."

Craig and Jake began to understand that their company's struggles started with them. They immediately went to work to right the ship. Craig and Jake transformed the way they trained salespeople and executed sales. Just like Brady holds detailed film sessions with his offense, Jake hosted a series of informational sessions that broke down the aeronautical design of their cranes in a language non-engineers could understand. He demonstrated to the sales team exactly why their cranes were so much more efficient, how the materials they used were more resistant to the elements, and more. He explained what all the specs meant, why they mattered, and what that meant for customers. Jake provided them with charts of just how much money and time a customer would save in the long run by purchasing their products, even if they were more expensive up front.

The sales team was stunned and delighted. They'd heard Craig and Jake say their cranes were better than the competitions', but they had no idea they were *that* much better. Based on what they learned in these presentations, the salespeople found new inspiration in their pitch to customers. Once they fully understood the cranes, they were much more convincing to customers. Their enthusiasm was infectious, and customers responded to the confidence the salespeople expressed.

Next, Craig, Jake, and Dan reworked the company's marketing materials. Instead of simply laying out the crane specs, they designed side-by-side comparisons of their cranes versus those of competitors. To ensure the customers understood the impact of the numbers, they included graphics, cost savings, and industry standards to illustrate exactly how superior their cranes were.

Craig and Jake shared the new marketing materials with the sales team and explained them in detail. They also took the opportunity to remind the team how strongly they believed in them and how they were so integral in moving the company down the path to success. They encouraged salespeople to come to them with any questions or difficulties they encountered. It was a level of open communication and encouragement the sales team had never before experienced.

Finally, Craig, Jake, and Dan crafted a plan to attract customers away from the dominating industry leaders. They made specialized marketing materials for those customers, including easy-to-understand direct comparisons between their products and those of the customers' current manufacturers. The materials especially targeted the competitors' weaknesses and highlighted how their cranes solved the issue seamlessly. This helped the sales team approach competitors' customers with confidence and pride. Previously, the salespeople would approach them timidly, proposing just a small segment of business. Instead, Craig and Jake instructed them to go in with the expectation that the customers would be so impressed with their cranes, they would want to switch manufacturers altogether. And now that the salespeople believed so strongly in the products, they could do so authentically.

The changes Craig and Jake introduced were game changers for the company. Within eight months, the company lured six of ten "dream clients" away from competitors. Orders exploded, and they even had trouble meeting production requirements. In fact, they had to manufacture cranes in the parking lot outside their facility until a larger factory was built. The company was so successful that they put one industry leader out of business and forced another to stop making boat cranes. Just like Brady invested in his teammates and demonstrated his belief in them, Craig and Jake transformed the attitude and approach of the sales team. With a clear understanding of the quality of their products, a strong self-belief, and engaged and encouraging leadership, the company grew into an industry leader.

GAME REVIEW:

- Great leaders don't expect their teams to figure out everything on their own. They don't assume team members will be able to execute a plan without teaching, preparation, and practice. Instead, they take a hands-on approach and work with the team until they're confident the team can perform at a high level.
- Even a great plan is more difficult to complete if those on the front line don't feel leadership has faith in them. The best teams are effective because their leaders believe in them and remind them frequently. Feeling a leader has confidence in the team is an important motivational tool.

EXECUTING THE PLAY

Exercises for the Preseason:

- How does your leadership style change when your team is under pressure? Evaluate what you do differently, how you react, and what you expect of your team. Are these moves reactionary, or are they designed in advance, and with a particular end in mind? What attitude do you exude when you're under pressure? You should have a crisis plan in place that informs how you behave during challenging times.

- Ultimately, every team sells something. Some teams sell widgets while others spread influence. What does your team "sell"? If you're the designated team leader, do you sense your team believes in its product? Does the team feel your support? If you're a member of the team, how do you feel about the product? What can you do to convince teammates and clients that the product is worthy?

- Do you believe in your team? If not, is your hesitation because of the team members, or because of the game plan? Alternatively, is your doubt in them related to a lack of confidence in your own leadership abilities? Try to identify where the block is and brainstorm methods to move past it.

Best Practices for the Game:

- It's one thing to believe in your team, but it's another thing to make sure they know it, without making them cocky. Explore new methods of motivating your teammates, particularly during times of struggle. What can you do to inspire their confidence while still reinforcing the importance of continued diligent preparation? Have fun with it!

- During times of stress, emotions often run high, which can harm team camaraderie. Watch for signs of this the next time your team is under pressure. Do what you can to deflect and diffuse tension and keep everyone focused on executing the game plan. Remind them that their excellent preparation makes them well equipped to handle anything that comes their way.

CHAPTER 12

Live the Image

"There's other things happening in my life, too. I do have kids that I love, and I don't want to be a dad that's not there driving my kids to their games. I think my kids have brought a great perspective in my life because kids just want the attention. You better be there and be available to them, or else they're going to look back on their life and go, 'Dad didn't really care that much.'"[1]
—Tom Brady

TOO GOOD TO BE TRUE?

By all accounts, Tom Brady has a beautiful life. He grew up in California in a happy, athletic family, went to private school, and was a two-sport star in high school. He went to a university elite in both academics and athletics and led his team to two bowl game victories. He plays the most important position in the most popular game in American sports. He's earned tens of millions of dollars as he's led his team to six Super Bowl championships and garnered three league MVPs. Athletic success and sponsorships have made him a global celebrity. He's tall and handsome and happily married to a supermodel. He has three children and seems to be an engaged father.

He is, in short, eminently hateable.

Brady's got it all, and damnit, it's fun to detest someone so perfect. Brady is the golden boy GOAT. Even now that Brady's moved on, New England worships him—as if Red Sox fans weren't bad enough. He's too good-looking and too successful for any one man. Schadenfreude feels extra delicious when Brady is the object. It's easy to be jealous, but this is much deeper than that: this is loathing at its most profound. And perhaps the worst thing about Brady is that he's so well liked by those who know him.

Most football players are, by necessity, emotional people. The game demands a player's whole life: mind, body, spirit, and time. Players must psych themselves up to play, regardless of weather or circumstance, to absorb vicious hits and deliver their own. It's a brutal game that requires a relentless spirit and never-say-die attitude. Many players have chips on their shoulders or lean on underdog mentalities to get an edge over the competition.

In such a passionate environment, it stands to reason that many players should hate Brady, just as many opposing fans do. Hatred would make it easier to avoid feeling intimidated by a player who has achieved so much success. It would give a player extra motivation to bring his A-game against Brady and his team. Furthermore, in a league where the average career lasts only about three years,[2] many players could benefit from the media attention a hot take on Brady would provide. The press, too, would no doubt love to break a scandalous story about the golden boy.

Brady is a man with the world at his fingertips. If he desired, he could treat teammates badly, disrespect his coaches, belittle his opponents, and brush off reporters. He's so talented and has been so successful that many people probably would not think twice about it. They would excuse his behavior as the price of excellence, or explain it away with the idea that men cannot be both great and good.

Some in the public assume Brady is a jerk when they see him lose his cool on the sidelines or feel he's aloof because he reveals so little to the press. Yet almost no players have a bad word to say about him. There's no doubt some of them dislike him, or are jealous as many fans are. Surely some former teammates are bitter at being released and would love to damage the the reputation of Brady's team. Occasionally you may hear a player comment that it's time people stop hero-worshipping him.[3]

But for the most part, even Brady's fiercest opponents can't help but respect him. Moreover, his current and former teammates adore him. Similarly, the press generally can't find much negative to publish about him. And there's simply too little information available to assume there's a darker story lurking somewhere. How is it that someone so hateable can be so well liked and embarrassment-free?

What comes out of the locker room time and again is praise of Brady. The stories are always about how friendly he is, how welcoming to new players, how he's one of the guys. He pushes himself harder than anyone and is always willing to put in extra work or tutoring with teammates who need help. Brady is said to treat people well, even reporters,[4] and to bring a good attitude every day. In person, he matches the image he puts out to the public.

The respect and camaraderie Brady enjoys in the NFL is a testament to his leadership and personality. In the NFL, it's easy for star players to be prima donnas. If you have enough talent, teams will put up with a great deal of bad behavior. Brady has never been known to cause a locker room problem. The media silence around Brady is the result of a man who generally practices what he preaches, exercises self-control, and keeps his priorities in check. Brady never forgets that his job is to lead his team to victory each and every week. Whatever he needs to do to make that happen, he will do. He leads by example and never loses focus.

Notice that Brady is no shrinking violet. His teammates approach him for advice because they know he will give them honest feedback that will make them better. Sometimes, that requires delivering harsh news. If a receiver isn't running a route properly, or an offensive lineman is getting outmaneuvered, Brady tells them. He doesn't do it cruelly, but he doesn't pull punches either, and his teammates respect his candor. They know he wouldn't bother putting in the time to help them improve if he didn't think they were capable of achieving it.

Of course, there are scandals—Spygate and Deflategate are very, very serious.[5] By any measure, they're a stain on his career and legacy. But in both cases, he denied all wrongdoing, and no one was ever able to definitively tie him to explicit wrongdoing. Even when it was rumored he orchestrated the trade of his backup Jimmy Garoppolo, Garoppolo has nothing but good things to say about Brady.[6] Now, maybe all of this is the result of luck, or an improper abuse of power, or a league that would rather have its most famous player's reputation remain mostly unscathed. Still, scandals fade with time and interpretation,[7] particularly as Brady keeps performing.

Scandals also haven't dimmed his popularity in the league. His teammates would still run through a wall for him. The NFL is a small enough community that if Brady were unpleasant to work with, word would spread. And still, players line up to sign with his team. Brady makes all of this possible by working to ensure his personality matches his reputation. He embraces the role he plays and lives the image he portrays.

LEADERSHIP LESSONS FROM THE FIELD:

- Leaders pay attention to how they are perceived. It matters how others view them. Effective leaders ensure they behave in a way that encourages strong relationships and builds trust.
- Simultaneously, leaders understand that authenticity is a key element of successful communication and solid teamwork. Observers can see though inauthenticity quickly, particularly when they spend as much time together as teammates do. The best leaders are careful to behave as their good reputation suggests they will.
- Even the most successful leaders make mistakes, or even get caught up in scandals. They don't have to be perfect, but they must lead by example the vast majority of the time. Otherwise, their reputations will be diminished, hindering their ability to lead.

Brady understands what so many business leaders have learned: leaders need to be likeable, authentic, and consistent. A crack in any of these attributes can damage an image irreparably. In fact, authentic leadership is a key predictor of an employee's job satisfaction, commitment to the organization, and workplace happiness.[8] Therefore, Brady works hard to project a certain image to the public. He knows that much of the country dislikes him and understands that success can be fleeting.

Brady's pristine image is what allows him goodwill in New England and Tampa and such lucrative global endorsements. In a society where so many people are desperate for attention, willing to expose every facet of their lives, Brady's image is carefully calculated. It's no wonder he has a team dedicated to his social media (see Chapter 9). Indeed, lots of athletes and celebrities attempt to create a positive public face for the benefits that persona generates. What makes him different from other celebrities is that by all available accounts, Brady truly lives the image he projects.

Brady is human, and humans have bad habits, foibles, and imperfections. He has a personal and professional life just like anybody else and faces stress in both. He makes mistakes. That Brady manages to keep his flaws so innocuous or under wraps is a testament to his self-control and to the way he treats people and develops relationships. Besides the occasional sideline rage, or shortness with the press if they talk about his family in a way he doesn't like,[9] he doesn't reveal many damning personality traits. Further, no one who has ever been around Brady reveals anything of consequence, which at the very least means he's earned their respect enough to keep quiet about whatever they don't love. Brady may be hated by much of the country, but he's about as squeaky clean as they come.

It's hard to get ahead if everyone thinks you're an asshole. When a leader is challenging to work with, the team's performance usually suffers. A difficult personality develops a reputation, which makes potential teammates not want to work with that person and makes other teams approach collaboration or competition with distrust. Brady, on the other hand, has players lining up to work with him and a following of former teammates who sing his praises. Brady works hard to create a positive public image and works even harder to ensure it's a real reflection of him.

Brady also understands that he has a very specific role to fill on his team, and he does everything he can to ensure he does that to the best of his abilities.

ACTION FROM THE BUSINESS STADIUM: UNDERSTANDING YOUR ROLE

Business coach Dan Larson told the story of a client that manufactured truck lighting. The CEO brought Dan in to support the aftermarket sales division, which had been experiencing declining sales and recently had a new division director. The CEO had faith in Grace, the new director, but also knew she would need support as she adjusted to the new role. Dan immediately set up a meeting with Grace.

"It's a pleasure to meet you, Grace. Your CEO tells me great things about you. He says you're very capable," Dan offered.

"Well, that's nice of him, but I have a lot to learn," Grace asserted. "We're facing a ton of offshore competition. Plus, I've managed a sales team before, but I've never managed a team of managers. I really want to get this right."

"I'm here to help. You're right to understand that managing a team of salespeople is different from managing a team of sales managers. The thing to remember is this: the team you're managing now has a very different purpose than the teams you've managed in the past. Before, you needed to make your team members great salespeople. Now, you need to make them great *leaders*," Dan said.

Dan explained that Grace, like Brady, needed to focus on how best to prepare her team to fulfill its designated function. He described, "It doesn't matter whether your direct reports are good salespeople. It matters that they can form a high-performance team in sales. They need to be good leaders. A good manager is part cheerleader, part butt-kicker."

Like Brady, Grace had to lead by example and live the image to which she wanted them to aspire. She immediately went to work. Drawing on her experience leading sales teams, she made a playbook. Only this time, the scripts, responses to common challenges, and sales materials were designed to help her team of managers. Just like salespeople working to sell to clients, her managers needed playbooks to create and maintain high-performance teams. She helped the managers organize contests and incentives to excite the salespeople and build camaraderie. Grace also convinced senior-level management to invest in a leadership development program to support her managers.

Like Brady, Grace was focused on helping her team achieve goals, individually and as a group. Whatever support they needed, she was prepared to give. Her team of managers immediately took to the training. Like many of Brady's new teammates, they had never received such comprehensive, personal support from a leader so generous with their time. Grace's enthusiasm kept them inspired and made them comfortable approaching her for help.

A few of Grace's managers needed more support than others. One manager, Ryan, was an excellent salesperson, but had never led a sales team before. His team was meeting their target sales numbers, but more because of Ryan's ability to sell than the team's collective effort. Grace set up a meeting with Ryan to see how she could help.

"Ryan, you're a great salesman, and a real go-getter. I see you putting in the extra time to make sales when your team is lagging a bit behind. You're meeting your numbers, but I worry that it's not happening as efficiently as it should. What do you see from your end?" Grace asked.

"It's been frustrating," admitted Ryan. "I've tried to share with them some of what's made me successful, but they just don't seem to take to it right away. And there's just not enough time to devote to it. If I give them more remedial help, then I won't have time to make the sales we need to hit our target. And when I do try to help, they don't seem to respond to me very well. I'm not sure they actually like me very much."

"Hmm. Why don't you give me a breakdown of your time?" suggested Grace.

"I spend probably thirty percent of my time with my team, reviewing their sales, giving them tips, helping them generate leads. Then another ten percent managing data and attending meetings. The other sixty percent is really all sales," Ryan shared.

"I see," replied Grace. "So look, you know I've never managed a team of sales managers before. It's been a tough adjustment. What I've learned in this new position is that my job *isn't* to be a good sales manager. My number one priority is to make you and your colleagues great *leaders*. In turn, you need to understand that your job isn't to be a great salesperson. It's to be a great manager of your team."

"OK, I hear you, but what does that look like?" asked Ryan.

"You spend more than half of your time selling, but you're not supposed to be a salesman. You're actively taking away time from what you should be doing, which is leading your team and making them the best at what they need to be doing. You need to pretty dramatically alter your time prioritization. It's a tough mental shift to make when you've spent your whole career excelling at sales, but it's what your team needs from you," said Grace.

"Think of the way you described the time you spend with them—you called it 'remedial help.' If that's the attitude you bring to training, they're going to see it on your face and feel it in how you teach. You need to transform how you view it, because it's the single most important part of your job. And by stepping in all the time to make sales, you're indirectly telling them that you don't believe they can do it on their own," she warned.

"If, instead, you invest time in your salespeople—in-depth, substantial time—your effort will pay off many times over.

When you really make sure they understand their sales playbooks, can execute the best practices and tactics you used, and approach their clients with confidence, you create a sales team full of little Ryans. Think of the potential of that group!" smiled Grace.

"And think about this too—putting in time with them is also sending a message that you believe in them, that they're capable and worth the effort. They'll feel empowered and encouraged. And that feeling will only grow as they see the results," she enthused. "Go be a *leader*."

After his conversation with Grace, Ryan reevaluated his approach and discovered a new vigor for his job. He knew the members of his team were smart and capable, so he had assumed they would just figure it out. Grace reminded him that he, too, needed help in the beginning. His team could do it, but they needed his support, not his interference.

Ryan developed one training session to teach his team his favorite sales techniques, and another to go over the sales playbook in detail. He had them role-play practice sales calls and offered honest, helpful feedback. Ryan started regularly meeting with each salesperson individually to monitor their progress and find ways he could support them. His team demonstrated immediate progress. Ryan started spending far less time selling, and his team's numbers continued to rise. Like Brady, Ryan inspired his team by his own performance and demonstrated his belief in them by investing the time they needed.

Grace and Ryan learned that they needed to understand and embrace their roles in the organization. Brady understands that he is the team leader, and as such, he has responsibilities that go beyond simply throwing the ball. He needs to ensure all players are on the same page, understand their responsibilities, and are fully prepared to execute at a high level. Similarly, Grace and Ryan learned that their teams needed a particular type of support they weren't accustomed to giving. They had to learn how to fulfill their duties and lead by example.

GAME REVIEW:

- The most effective leaders understand that not all teams have the same function, and thus don't have the same needs. Leaders need to adjust their communication, support, and expectations based on the responsibility their team needs to fulfill.
- Authenticity is key to leadership. If you feel burdened by your team, your teammates likely can tell. They need to feel your faith in their ability to succeed. Demonstrate it in word and deed.

EXECUTING THE PLAY

Exercises for the Preseason:

- Consider your company's core values and ethos you encourage within your team. How well do you personally embody them? If an observer didn't know those goals, would that person be able to identify them by examining your conduct? If not, brainstorm how you could exhibit them in meaningful ways.
- Are you kind? Do you treat people with respect? Are you willing to go the extra mile for a teammate when it would help achieve the greater goal? If you're not sure, ask yourself whether people approach you for help or advice, or whether they avoid you when they can. (Also remember that kindness is not the same as niceness; niceness can be your worst enemy. Visit bit.ly/KDNice for more information.)

Best Practices for the Game:

- Leaders work to make sure they are relatable and authentic. The next time it's relevant, share with your team the story of a time you failed. Describe what the consequences were, how you felt, and what you did to overcome the disappointment. Your team will appreciate the reminder of your humanity and will see you as an ally in their effort to grow and improve.

- Authenticity requires honesty. When teammates come to you for feedback on a project, do you dismiss them with a noncommittal, "It's fine," or do you dig deeper to find how their performance could be improved? Your teammates show you respect by seeking your counsel; demonstrate your respect for them by helping them raise their level.

Epilogue

In the spring of 2020, Tom Brady announced he would leave the New England Patriots to join the Tampa Bay Buccaneers.[1] Although the leadership stories in this book are based on Brady's time with the Patriots, even his leaving demonstrated his penchant for being a leader. In departing New England, some might say he turned his back on an organization that gave him so much or revealed ego-driven motives. Those assessments can still be true without necessarily taking away from the leadership skill he demonstrated while switching teams. In fact, Brady demonstrated strong leadership throughout the process. He said all the right things in the lead-up to free agency,[2] and once it was official he was leaving New England, he said all the right things about his experience there, the people he loved, everything he learned, and his deep gratitude.[3]

In a fascinating and revealing interview with Howard Stern, Brady shared why he chose the Buccaneers. His thought process exhibited the same careful planning and devotion to team success he's displayed throughout his career. The Bucs appealed to him because of the opportunity they presented: a solid team with a group of highly skilled receivers,[4] a bright, well-liked coaching staff,[5] and the chance to play in a warm climate.[6] Perhaps most important, however, was Tampa Bay's relative proximity to his eldest son, who lives in New York. As always, Brady's holistic approach to decision-making accounted for both his professional and personal life and included a thorough analysis of the team.

Brady's negotiations with the Buccaneers also exhibited deft leadership. He never asked Tampa Bay brass about the skills of the receivers on the team or how the coaching staff imagined running the offense. Instead, Brady asked whether the receivers were "good guys."[7] Brady did all necessary research in preparation for the meeting, so that he could use the meeting to focus on important intangibles like personality.[8] He also never demanded a say in personnel decisions or offensive strategy, but rather asked for the phone numbers of all his new teammates.[9]

When he officially joined Tampa Bay, Brady faced his new challenge with enthusiasm.[10] Receiver Chris Godwin—sure to be one of Brady's primary receiving targets—already had jersey number 12, and although much of Brady's marketing revolved around using that jersey number, he didn't ask or pressure Godwin to change numbers (although admittedly it was an elephant in a very public room). When Godwin volunteered to give Brady his preferred number, Brady thanked him publicly.[11]

It is also interesting to note that Rob Gronkowski, one of Brady's favorite targets in New England, seemed to come out of retirement specifically to rejoin Brady.[12] While Gronk didn't directly say Brady was the reason he returned, Gronk did say he would have considered any team where Brady signed.[13] Gronkowski was having a ton of fun in retirement,[14] and surely Brady demands a great deal from his favorite tight end. Playing with Brady again must have been a powerful draw for the fun-loving Gronk to end a year-long party.

Brady's ultimate legacy is not yet written in stone. There's little doubt he will face tough adjustments with a new team and a different system, but there's also little doubt that Brady will attack these challenges with the same belief, dedication, and leadership he's always presented. No one knows what will happen in Tampa Bay, but Brady's remarkable leadership skill will certainly light the path to success.

About the Authors

Kevin Daum is an entrepreneur, author, and speaker who has engaged and inspired audiences around the globe. A serial entrepreneur with multiple successful exits, Kevin built an Inc. 500 company, where his sales and marketing techniques resulted in more than $1 billion in sales. Kevin is the award-winning author of several Amazon bestselling books, including *ROAR! Get Heard in the Sales and Marketing Jungle* and *Video Marketing for Dummies*, and he was a major contributor to the bestseller *Scaling Up*. Kevin's column on Inc. com garners more than 200,000 hits per month, and he hosts the podcast *10 Minute Tips from the Top*, where he interviews CEOs of the world's most prestigious companies. He's also the media expert in residence and New York ambassador of International Deal Gateway.

Kevin is a graduate of the MIT Entrepreneurial Executive Leadership program and was a longtime member of Entrepreneur's Organization, where he held several board positions and founded the Silicon Valley chapter. Kevin was a three-time winner of EO's Global Learning Award. He has facilitated unique arts-based learning programs for Fortune 500 companies and was instrumental in the development of interdisciplinary arts and entrepreneurship curriculum at Baylor University. He lectures regularly at Columbia University and coaches senior executives on leadership communication through multimedia.

A strong believer in the arts, Kevin has a theatre degree from Humboldt State University. Kevin also has an MS in media management from Fordham University, where he teaches media and entrepreneurship as an adjunct professor. He resides in New York City.

Anne Mary Ciminelli is an associate editor at TAE International, where she conducts research, writes, copyedits, and manages projects. She also has experience consulting for small businesses as they construct business plans, explore partnership opportunities, and apply for funding grants.

Anne Mary is a graduate of the Walsh School of Foreign Service at Georgetown University. She also holds an MBA and a JD from Fordham University. She lives in Potomac, Maryland.

Endnotes

CHAPTER 1

1. https://www.instagram.com/p/B1KoCFhhDYX/ and https://sports.yahoo.com/tom-brady-calls-out-patriots-rookie-on-instagram-study-your-playbook-171820765.html
2. http://www.thepostgame.com/blog/more-family-fun/201202/sister-pact-how-tom-bradys-special-bond-his-sisters-helped-make-him-star
3. https://www.nydailynews.com/sports/football/giants/story-boy-named-tom-brady-article-1.341686
4. https://www.nydailynews.com/sports/football/giants/story-boy-named-tom-brady-article-1.341686
5. http://www.thepostgame.com/blog/more-family-fun/201202/sister-pact-how-tom-bradys-special-bond-his-sisters-helped-make-him-star
6. https://www.boston.com/sports/new-england-patriots/2016/11/20/when-tom-brady-was-a-linebacker
7. https://www.boston.com/sports/new-england-patriots/2016/11/20/when-tom-brady-was-a-linebacker
8. https://www.si.com/vault/2012/01/09/106148035/tom-brady-as-you-forgot-him
9. https://www.cbssports.com/nfl/news/tom-brady-explains-what-a-day-in-the-life-of-tom-brady-is-like/
10. https://www.maxpreps.com/news/85CGqLN9i0mLFr7AwfXqNA/tom-brady-was-no-goody-two-shoes-at-serra-high-school.htm
11. https://www.stack.com/a/tom-bradys-high-school-footwork-drill-laid-the-foundation-for-super-bowl-success and https://bleacherreport.com/articles/2691611-tom-bradys-latest-act-of-greatness-was-a-lifetime-in-the-making and https://www.nydailynews.com/sports/football/giants/story-boy-named-tom-brady-article-1.341686

12. https://www.nydailynews.com/sports/football/giants /story-boy-named-tom-brady-article-1.341686

13. https://www.maxpreps.com/news/85CGqLN9i0mLFr7Aw fXqNA/tom-brady-was-no-goody-two-shoes-at-serra-high -school.htm

14. https://tb12sports.com/blog/pliability

15. https://www.cbssports.com/nfl/news/tom-brady-explains-what -a-day-in-the-life-of-tom-brady-is-like/

16. https://www.psychologytoday.com/us/blog/flourish/200912 /seeing-is-believing-the-power-visualization

17. http://www.thepostgame.com/features/201101/tom -bradys-guruandhttps://www.insider.com/tom-brady-greg-harden -howard-stern-interview-2020-4

18. https://www.insider.com/tom-brady-greg-harden-howard -stern-interview-2020-4

19. https://tb12.brainhq.com/

20. https://www.washingtonpost.com/sports/2019/01/29 /secret-tom-bradys-longevity/

21. https://www.siriusdecisions.com/blog/the-three-degrees-of -guided-selling

22. https://aberdeen.canto.com/b/QBVQN

23. https://www.siriusdecisions.com/blog/its-time-for-activity -based-enablement

24. Daly, Jack and Dan Larson. *The Sales Playbook: for Hyper Sales Growth*. ForbesBooks 2016.

CHAPTER 2

1. https://twitter.com/TomBrady/status/1158113655944286209

2. 26 https://goleathernecks.com/news/2010/4/2/Rodney _Harrison_Named_to_Patriots_All_Decade_Team.aspx

3. https://bleacherreport.com/articles/192061-rodney -harrison-retires-after-15-years

4. http://nbcsportsgrouppressbox.com/bio/rodney-harrison/

5. https://goleathernecks.com/news/2010/4/2/Rodney _Named_to_Patriots_All_Decade_Team.aspx

6. https://www.espn.com/nfl/story/_/id/20222434/tom-brady -40th-birthday-stories-never-heard-nfl-2017-new-england- patriots

7. https://www.espn.com/nfl/story/_/id/20222434/tom-brady -40th-birthday-stories-never-heard-nfl-2017-new-england -patriots

8. https://www.businessinsider.com/tom-bradys-insane-compet itiveness-examples-2017-8#it-all-started-in-high-school-for -brady-he-used-to-have-his-high-school-teammates-over-his -house-to-study-film-while-his-mom-made-them-lunch-10

9. https://hbr.org/2015/02/increase-the-odds-of-achieving-your -goals-by-setting-them-with-your-spouse

10. https://www.dominican.edu/academics/lae/undergraduate -programs/psych/faculty/assets-gail-matthews/research summary2.pdf and https://www.psychologytoday.com/us/blog /the-moment-youth/201803/goal-setting-is-linked -higher-achievement

CHAPTER 3

1. https://www.foxsports.com/nfl/story/tom-brady-swears-during -postgame-press-conference-after-super-bowl-51-020517

2. https://www.pro-football-reference.com/teams/atl/2016.htm

3. https://www.pro-football-reference.com/awards/ap-nfl-mvp -award.htm

4. https://www.espn.com/nfl/playbyplay?gameId=400927752

5. https://www.pro-football-reference.com/leaders/pass_int_perc _career.htm

6. https://www.pro-football-reference.com/leaders/pick _six_career.htm and https://profootballtalk.nbcsports.com/2019 /06/29/aaron-rodgers-tom-brady-have-avoided-pick-sixes-like -no-other-quarterbacks/

7. https://www.espn.com/nfl/playbyplay?gameId=400927752

8. https://www.si.com/nfl/2017/02/05/super-bowl -biggest-comebacks-patriots

9. https://www.espn.com/nfl/playbyplay?gameId=400927752

10. https://www.msn.com/en-us/sports/nfl/the-top-15-qbs-who -have-the-most-fourth-quarter-comebacks-in-nfl-history /ar-BBNfnTT

11. https://www.espn.com/nfl/playbyplay?gameId=400927752

12. https://www.espn.com/nfl/playbyplay?gameId=400927752

13. https://www.si.com/nfl/2019/02/03/super-bowl -2019-overtime-patriots-falcons-tom-brady

14. https://www.foxsports.com/nfl/story/super-bowl-51-the-play -of-the-game-was-the-overtime-coin-toss-020617

15. https://www.espn.com/nfl/playbyplay?gameId=400927752

16. https://www.theringer.com/2017/2/6/16077576/nfl-playoffs -super-bowl-atlanta-falcons-new-england-patriots-tom-brady -goat-2782939d0909

17. https://www.sbnation.com/2017/2/6/14519000/tom-brady
    -super-bowl-mvp-press-conference-patriots-vs-falcons
18. https://www.health.harvard.edu/mind-and-mood/protect
    -your-brain-from-stress
19. https://hbr.org/2019/11/making-work-less-stressful-and-more
    -engaging-for-your-employees

CHAPTER 4

1. https://247sports.com/nfl/new-england-patriots/Article
    /Tom-Brady-Bill-Belichick-film-study-127889471/
2. https://www.espn.com/nfl/playoffs/2012/story/_/page
    /hotread-tom-brady/nfl-playoffs-tom-brady-eyes-backups
3. https://nesn.com/2020/04/tom-brady-on-howard-stern-live
    -recap-what-we-learned-from-qbs-interview/
4. https://hbr.org/2017/07/stop-the-meeting-madness
5. https://meeting-report.com/
6. Lencioni, Patrick. *Death By Meeting: A Leadership Fable.* Jossey
    -Bass, 2004.
7. Harnish, Verne. *Scaling Up.* Gazelles, Inc., 2014, 175.
8. https://hbr.org/2017/07/stop-the-meeting-madness
9. Harnish, 179–180.
10. EOS Worldwide. http://www.eosworldwide.com
11. BHAG © Jim Collins and Jerry I. Porras

CHAPTER 5

1. https://www.washingtonpost.com/sports/2019/01/12/hi-im-tom
    -brady-how-patriots-year-old-quarterback-relates-teammates/
2. http://www.nfl.com/news/story/0ap3000001106744/article
    /tom-brady-finalizes-agreement-to-join-buccaneers
3. https://www.msn.com/en-us/sports/nfl/highest-paid-quarter
    backs-ranking-nfl-qbs-by-salary-for-2019-season/ar-BBUsTs2
    and https://www.sportingnews.com/us/nfl/news/nfl-highest-paid
    -quarterbacks-salary/19ff2askk3p2f1p2fct7yd49lx
4. https://www.nbcsports.com/boston/patriots/tom-bradys
    -patriots-contracts-through-years
5. https://www.nbcsports.com/boston/patriots/tom-bradys
    -patriots-contracts-through-years
6. https://twitter.com/DonteStallworth/status/65137545
    1789729792
7. https://www.espn.com/boston/nfl/story/_/id/12272310/tom
    -brady-new-england-patriots-plans-give-mvp-truck-malcolm
    -butler

8. https://news.gallup.com/poll/241649/employee-engagement-rise.aspx

9. https://news.gallup.com/poll/241649/employee-engagement-rise.aspx

10. https://news.gallup.com/reports/191489/q12-meta-analysis-report-2016.aspx

11. https://nypost.com/2019/05/03/tom-brady-on-modest-contract-im-selfless-and-my-wife-makes-a-lot-of-money/?utm_medium=SocialFlow&sr_share=facebook&utm_campaign=Social Flow&utm_source=NYPFacebook and https://www.youtube.com/watch?v=R4QLk-jATZs

12. https://www.businessinsider.com/ceos-who-take-1-dollar-salary-or-less-2015-8

13. https://jackdalysales.com/about-jack/

CHAPTER 6

1. https://weei.radio.com/blogs/mike-petraglia/tom-brady-beating-rams-super-bowl-it-doesnt-seem-long-ago

2. https://www.pro-football-reference.com/teams/nyj/2006.htm

3. https://www.wsj.com/articles/SB10001424052748703805004575606942893014712

4. https://www.nydailynews.com/sports/football/chad-pennington-wins-nfl-comeback-player-year-award-article-1.420525

5. https://www.pro-football-reference.com/boxscores/200701070nwe.htm

6. https://www.pro-football-reference.com/teams/nyj/2007.htm

7. https://www.pro-football-reference.com/teams/nyj/2006_roster.htm
https://www.pro-football-reference.com/players/R/ReviDa99/gamelog/2007/
https://www.espn.com/nfl/trainingcamp07/news/story?id=2976504

8. http://sports.espn.go.com/nfl/news/story?id=3272497
http://sports.espn.go.com/nfl/news/story?id=3275059
http://sports.espn.go.com/nfl/news/story?id=3275142

9. https://www.nydailynews.com/sports/football/jets/jets-leave-plenty-stories-behind-hempstead-article-1.317784

10. https://www.pro-football-reference.com/players/F/FavrBr00.htm

11. https://www.espn.com/nfl/scoreboard/_/year/2007/seasontype/3/week/3

12. https://web.archive.org/web/20081001090907/http://ap
.google.com/article/ALeqM5jvw9T8npvObo
HqSZiNwpRjOprtwAD93FV9V01
13. https://www.pro-football-reference.com/teams/nyj/2008.htm
14. https://www.espn.com/blog/new-york-jets/post/_/id/76874
/brett-the-jet-recalling-the-trade-that-demanded-11-exclamation
-points
15. https://www.nytimes.com/2008/12/29/sports/football/29
araton.html
16. http://nymag.com/intelligencer/2008/12/finally_thats_over
_the_jets_ma.html
17. https://www.espn.com/nfl/news/story?id=3808669&
campaign=rss&source=ESPNHeadlines
https://web.archive.org/web/20090502080111/http://myespn
.go.com/blogs/afceast/0-7-169/Jets-release-Favre—clear-way
-for-possible-return.html
18. https://nypost.com/2016/09/27/inside-eric-manginis-jets-tenure
-favre-arm-twist-2-faced-owner-spygate-regret/
19. https://nypost.com/2016/09/27/inside-eric-manginis-jets-tenure
-favre-arm-twist-2-faced-owner-spygate-regret/
20. https://www.espn.com/blog/new-york-jets/post/_/id/76874
/brett-the-jet-recalling-the-trade-that-demanded-11-exclamation
-points
21. https://nypost.com/2008/08/19/favre-still-trying-to-digest
-jets-offense/
22. https://www.espn.com/blog/new-york-jets/post/_/id/76874
/brett-the-jet-recalling-the-trade-that-demanded-11-exclamation
-points
https://www.nbcnewyork.com/news/sports/fanho-brett
-favre-implores-eric-mangini-please-dumb-down-the-jets-offense
/1844480/
https://www.nytimes.com/2008/12/31/sports/football/31jets
.html
23. https://web.archive.org/web/20090508053513/http://www
.nfl.com/gamecenter/recap?game_id=29533&displayPage=tab
_recap&season=2008&week=REG1
24. https://web.archive.org/web/20090307054122/http://www
.nfl.com/gamecenter/playbyplay?game_id=29533&displayPage
=tab_play_by_play&season=2008&week=REG1&override=true
25. http://archive.boston.com/sports/football/patriots/articles
/2008/09/10/sources_brady_tore_acl_and_mcl/

26. https://www.yahoo.com/news/cassel-finally-gets-shot
-214300504—nfl.html

27. https://www.theringer.com/nfl/2018/8/9/17670364/new
-england-patriots-2008-season-tom-brady-injury-matt-cassel
-bill-belichick

28. https://www.theringer.com/nfl/2018/8/9/17670364/new
-england-patriots-2008-season-tom-brady-injury-matt-cassel
-bill-belichick

29. http://archive.boston.com/sports/football/patriots
/articles/2008/09/10/sources_brady_tore_acl_and_mcl/

30. https://www.si.com/vault/2009/06/01/105819805/ive-done
-everything-i-could-to-push-myself-sometimes-too-hard
-right-now-im-doing-everything-theres-nothing-i-cant-do

31. http://www.espn.com/espn/wire/_/section/nfl/id/3771873 and
http://www.espn.com/espn/wire/_/section/nfl/id/3796960

32. https://medium.com/crowdbotics/hips-dont-lie-15-project
-management-stats-you-can-t-ignore-6f655060ef30

33. https://medium.com/crowdbotics/hips-dont-lie-15-project
-management-stats-you-can-t-ignore-6f655060ef30

34. https://hive.com/blog/project-management-statistics/

CHAPTER 7

1. https://www.patriots.com/news/transcript-tom-brady-9-4

2. https://www.washingtonpost.com/sports/2019/01/12/hi-im
-tom-brady-how-patriots-year-old-quarterback-relates-team
mates/ among many others

3. http://www.startribune.com/patriots-get-rich-on-inexpensive
-talent-tailor-made-for-their-system/412800113/

4. https://bleacherreport.com/articles/1399397-patriots-league
-leaders-at-taking-chances-with-players

5. http://uli.org/wp-content/uploads/ULI-Documents/The
-Human-Era-at-Work.pdf and https://hbr.org/2016/07/a-global
-survey-on-the-ambiguous-state-of-employee-trust

6. https://hbr.org/2017/01/the-neuroscience-of-trust

7. https://www.si.com/nfl/2017/01/16/tom-brady-receivers
-brotherhood-patriots-michigan

CHAPTER 8

1. *Tom vs Time*, https://www.religionofsports.com/content/tom-vs
-time/

2. https://www.usatoday.com/story/sports/nfl/2015/10/28/list-of-notable-practice-squad-graduates/74726098/
3. https://www.ajc.com/sports/football/look-nfl-new-practice-rules/ZLKiNsjADuSDy8uHzsvYoN/
4. https://nationalfootballpost.com/sources-say-tension-with-dolphins-had-been-mounting-for-weeks-in-practice/
5. https://bleacherreport.com/articles/2576553-donte-stallworth-says-tom-brady-used-to-pay-practice-squad-players-for-ints
6. https://youtu.be/V74AxCqOTvg

CHAPTER 9

1. http://archive.boston.com/sports/football/patriots/articles/2011/01/09/the_great_communicator/
2. https://sports.yahoo.com/michael-jordan-really-cut-high-school-team-215707476.html
3. https://www.patriots.com/news/new-england-patriots-2010-season-review-113741
4. https://www.pro-football-reference.com/players/B/BradTo00.htm
5. https://www.pro-football-reference.com/years/2010/
6. https://www.goodhousekeeping.com/life/entertainment/news/a47710/tom-brady-gisele-marriage/
7. https://www.espn.com/blog/nflnation/post/_/id/39177/tom-brady-cries-when-recalling-2000-draft
8. https://www.businessinsider.com/tom-brady-nfl-draft-quarterbacks-2017-2
9. https://www.facebook.com/TomBrady/photos/a.655314961176324/780683791972773/?type=3
10. https://www.facebook.com/TomBrady/photos/a.233362006704957/1169883299719485/?type=3&theater
11. https://www.facebook.com/facebookmedia/success-stories/tom-brady-uses-facebook-to-build-community-and-grow-business
12. https://www.washingtonpost.com/news/early-lead/wp/2015/09/10/it-takes-a-team-to-make-tom-bradys-facebook-page-so-amazing/
13. https://www.religionofsports.com/content/tom-vs-time/
14. https://www.facebook.com/facebookmedia/success-stories/tom-brady-uses-facebook-to-build-community-and-grow-business
15. https://www.amazon.com/gp/product/1501180738/
16. https://www.ibm.com/cloud-computing/solutions/video/enterprise-video-for-internal-communications/ and https://everyonesocial.com/blog/internal-communications-statistics/

17. https://www.conference-board.org/topics/dna-of-engagement and https://everyonesocial.com/blog/internal-communications -statistics/
18. https://www.psychologytoday.com/us/blog/inside-the -consumer-mind/201302/how-emotions-influence-what -we-buy
19. https://www.nbcsports.com/boston/patriots/matt-cassel -details-patriots-prank-war-led-tom-brady-pee-his-practice -jersey
20. https://www.harvardbusiness.org/what-makes-storytelling -so-effective-for-learning/

CHAPTER 10

1. https://985thesportshub.com/2020/01/08/tom-brady-has-a -long-heartfelt-message-for-patriots-fans-on-instagram/
2. https://www.espn.com/nfl/story/_/id/14286587/how-patriots -malcolm-butler-made-greatest-play-super-bowl-history-beat -seahawks
3. https://www.pro-football-reference.com/players/B/ButlMa01 .htm
4. https://www.espn.com/nfl/story/_/id/14286587/how-patriots -malcolm-butler-made-greatest-play-super-bowl-history-beat -seahawks
5. https://www.espn.com/nfl/story/_/id/14286587/how-patriots -malcolm-butler-made-greatest-play-super-bowl-history-beat -seahawks
6. https://www.pro-football-reference.com/players/L/LyncMa00 .htm
7. https://985thesportshub.com/2018/02/01/reminder-malcolm -butler-made-several-great-plays-super-bowl-xlix/
8. https://985thesportshub.com/2018/02/01/reminder-malcolm -butler-made-several-great-plays-super-bowl-xlix/
9. https://www.espn.com/nfl/playbyplay?gameId=400749027
10. https://985thesportshub.com/2018/02/01/reminder-malcolm -butler-made-several-great-plays-super-bowl-xlix/
11. https://985thesportshub.com/2018/02/01/reminder-malcolm -butler-made-several-great-plays-super-bowl-xlix/
12. https://www.espn.com/nfl/playbyplay?gameId=400749027
13. https://www.espn.com/nfl/playbyplay?gameId=400749027
14. https://www.espn.com/nfl/playbyplay?gameId=400749027
15. https://www.dailymotion.com/video/x2nl9or
16. https://www.youtube.com/watch?v=i96fPP37RyA

17. https://www.youtube.com/watch?v=i96fPP37RyA
18. http://www.nfl.com/news/story/0ap3000000467664
    /article/malcolm-butler-i-knew-what-was-going-to-happen
    and https://www.si.com/nfl/2016/02/02/super-bowl-49-ending
    -oral-history
19. https://www.espn.com/nfl/story/_/id/14286587/how-patriots
    -malcolm-butler-made-greatest-play-super-bowl-history-beat
    -seahawks
20. https://www.espn.com/nfl/playbyplay?gameId=400749027
21. https://www.espn.com/nfl/playbyplay?gameId=400749027
22. http://www.nfl.com/news/story/0ap3000000468077/article
    /malcolm-butler-a-late-substitution-on-gamewinner
23. https://deadspin.com/the-patriots-knew-exactly-what-was
    -coming-1683211802
24. https://www.youtube.com/watch?v=i96fPP37RyA
25. https://bleacherreport.com/articles/2599007-inside-malcolm
    -butlers-journey-from-reject-prospect-to-revis-replacement
26. http://insidethepylon.com/film-study/film-study-nfl
    /defense-film-study-nfl/2015/09/10/do-your-job-the-goal-line/
27. https://www.caranddriver.com/news/a15357652/tom-brady
    -gives-malcolm-butler-the-mvp-chevy-colorado-he-deserves/
28. https://www.theguardian.com/sport/2015/feb/02/tom-brady
    -heaps-praise-on-malcolm-butler-after-super-bowl-interception
29. https://www.theringer.com/nfl-playoffs/2018/1/30/16949762
    /super-bowl-new-england-patriots-fourth-quarter-comebacks
    -running-conditioning
30. https://www.businessinsider.com/patriots-train-game
    -situations-advantage-2018-1
31. https://www.theringer.com/nfl-playoffs/2018/1/30/16949762
    /super-bowl-new-england-patriots-fourth-quarter-comebacks
    -running-conditioning
32. https://www.youtube.com/watch?v=i96fPP37RyA
33. http://ol.scc.spokane.edu/jroth/Courses/English%20
    94-study%20skills/MASTER%20DOCS%20and%20TESTS
    /Curve%20of%20Forgetting.htm
34. https://news.gallup.com/businessjournal/174197/managers
    -focus-performance-engagement.aspx

CHAPTER 11

1. https://www.nbcsports.com/boston/new-england-patriots
   /brady-reflects-how-motivate-patriots-teammates

2. https://www.pro-football-reference.com/players/J/JohnCh01.htm
3. https://www.cnbc.com/id/42749405
4. https://web.archive.org/web/20060904131006/http://msn.foxsports.com/other/story/5872400
5. http://www.nfl.com/news/story/09000d5d82abf2c7/article/dolphins-chad-ochocinco-changes-name-to-chad-johnson
6. https://www.cincinnati.com/story/sports/nfl/bengals/2018/01/09/mike-brown-marvin-lewis-fact-fiction-cincinnati-bengals-lack-discipline-accountability/1013728001/ and https://www.theringer.com/nfl/2018/12/31/18162996/marvin-lewis-cincinnati-bengals-fired
7. https://www.espn.com/boston/nfl/story/_/id/6815893/chad-ochocinco-new-england-patriots-camp-trade-official
8. https://bleacherreport.com/articles/785898-chad-ochocinco-his-social-media-empire-the-patriots-way
9. https://www.foxsports.com/nfl/story/new-england-patriots-tom-brady-bill-belichick-chad-johnson-meeting-102516
10. https://www.foxsports.com/nfl/story/new-england-patriots-tom-brady-bill-belichick-chad-johnson-meeting-102516
11. https://patriotswire.usatoday.com/2017/09/17/what-its-like-to-study-film-with-bill-belichick/
12. https://patriotswire.usatoday.com/2017/09/17/what-its-like-to-study-film-with-bill-belichick/
13. http://www.nfl.com/news/story/0ap3000000728192/article/ochocinco-belichicks-brady-rant-put-me-on-eggshells
14. https://www.espn.com/nfl/story/_/page/hotread180105/beginning-end-new-england-patriots-robert-kraft-tom-brady-bill-belichick-internal-power-struggle
15. http://www.nfl.com/news/story/0ap3000000728192/article/ochocinco-belichicks-brady-rant-put-me-on-eggshells
16. https://www.jimcollins.com/media_topics/TheStockdaleParadox.html

CHAPTER 12

1. https://www.businessinsider.com/tom-brady-gisele-bundchen-nfl-career-future-2018-6
2. https://www.wsj.com/articles/the-shrinking-shelf-life-of-nfl-players-1456694959
3. https://bleacherreport.com/articles/2338593-richard-sherman-speaks-on-tom-bradys-public-image-2012-in-game-comments

4. https://www.espn.com/nfl/story/_/id/28900439/tom-brady
   -new-england-kindness-leaves-lasting-impression-reporter
5. https://bleacherreport.com/articles/2337295-cheating-scandals
   -will-forever-tarnish-the-brady-belichick-legacy
6. https://bleacherreport.com/articles/2796599-jimmy-garoppolo
   -on-relationship-with-tom-brady-we-still-text-here-and-there
7. https://www.forbes.com/sites/alexreimer/2015/12/18
   /tom-brady-deflategate-and-donald-trump-friendship
   -are-overblown-scandals/#7c1c2f71f05b and https://profootball
   talk.nbcsports.com/2015/05/06/finally-the-halftime
   -psi-numbers-are-known/
8. https://blog.hubspot.com/marketing/authentic-leadership
   and https://www.researchgate.net/publication/228654971_
   Entrepreneurs_as_Authentic_Leaders_Impact_on_Employees'
   _Attitudes
9. https://abcnews.go.com/Sports/tom-brady-shows
   -compassion-radio-host-insulted-daughter/story?id=52698492

EPILOGUE

1. https://www.espn.com/nfl/story/_/id/28930366/tom
   -brady-says-signing-buccaneers
2. https://www.boston.com/sports/new-england-patriots
   /2020/03/13/tom-brady-free-agency-quotes
3. https://www.nbcsports.com/boston/patriots/tom-brady
   -announces-hes-leaving-patriots-free-agent-destination
   -unknown and https://www.insider.com/howard-stern-tom
   -brady-interview-best-moments-2020-4#brady-also-offered
   -some-insight-into-why-he-chose-to-go-to-tampa-bay-over
   -other-offers-citing-staying-close-to-family-warm-weather
   -and-head-coach-bruce-arians-as-key-factors-4
4. https://www.sbnation.com/nfl/2020/3/18/21184550
   /tom-brady-tampa-bay-buccaneers-wide-receivers-patriots
   -bruce-arians
5. https://nesn.com/2020/04/tom-brady-on-howard-stern-live
   -recap-what-we-learned-from-qbs-interview/
6. https://ftw.usatoday.com/2020/04/tom-brady
   -howard-stern-interview-belichick-gisele
7. https://www.tampabay.com/sports/bucs/2020/03/21/how-the
   -bucs-got-tom-brady-to-leave-the-new-england-patriots-for
   -tampa-bay/
8. 218 https://www.tampabay.com/sports/bucs/2020/03/21
   /how-the-bucs-got-tom-brady-to-leave-the-new-england

-patriots-for-tampa-bay/ and https://www.inc.com/jeff-haden/when-tom-brady-negotiated-his-new-contract-with-tampa-bay-buccaneers-only-special-request-he-made-is-a-lesson-in-emotional-intelligence.html

9. https://www.nbcsports.com/boston/patriots/tom-brady-had-just-one-request-after-signing-tampa-bay-buccaneers
10. https://www.instagram.com/p/B99KHG5hC_n/?igshid=1lpwjhocvy613
11. https://www.nbcsports.com/boston/patriots/how-tom-brady-thanked-bucs-chris-godwin-giving-him-no-12-free
12. https://sports.yahoo.com/rob-gronkowski-explains-why-he-came-back-what-he-weighs-and-his-thoughts-on-bill-belichick-202402235.html
13. https://www.facebook.com/watch/live/?v=531559484146044&ref=watch_permalink
14. https://clutchpoints.com/the-best-moments-of-rob-gronkowski-brief-retirement/